THE HANMOJI HANDBOOK

Your Guide to the Chinese Language Through Emoji

Jason Li, An Xiao Mina, and Jennifer 8. Lee

≡MiTeenPress

For Emmett, Lulu, and Madison

The MIT Press, the ≡MITeenPress colophon, and MITeen Press are trademarks
of The MIT Press, a department of the Massachusetts Institute of Technology,
and used under license from The MIT Press. The colophon and MITeen Press
are registered in the US Patent and Trademark Office.

First paperback edition 2023

Library of Congress Catalog Card Number 2021947885
ISBN 978-1-5362-1913-5 (hardcover)
ISBN 978-1-5362-3046-8 (paperback)

23 24 25 26 27 28 APS 10 9 8 7 6 5 4 3 2 1

Printed in Hong Kong

This book was typeset in Source Sans Pro, Source Serif Pro,
Noto Sans CJK, and Noto Emoji.

MITeen Press
an imprint of Candlewick Press
99 Dover Street
Somerville, Massachusetts 02144

miteenpress.com
candlewick.com

Contents

Introduction

Hi! 火 豬 水

▶ It's not every day a new writing system is born.

Emoji were developed in the late 1990s in Japan. Thanks to the spread of computers and mobile phones, emoji have traveled to the far reaches of the globe, and billions of them are sent across the internet every day, expressing joy, heartbreak, late-night snack cravings, and corny jokes. There are currently more than three thousand emoji, and many more are on the way.

Developed thousands of years ago and traditionally written with brushes, Chinese writing might seem to be a world away from the beeps and boops of online messages, but Chinese is one of the most popular languages online. More than eighty thousand Chinese characters are recognized in dictionaries, reflecting a long, diverse history of cultural evolution and writing.

What Chinese writing and emoji have in common is that they both convey meaning through images instead of an alphabet. Many of these images began as literal depictions of the world, from trees and birds to fire and water. Over time, both writing systems have evolved to suggest more complex concepts, like "that's lit" or "thank you."

We brought Chinese characters, or **hanzi** (漢字/汉子 *hànzì/hon3zi6*), and emoji together because, as lovers of languages, we enjoy exploring and playing with words. And what better way to do that than with one of the oldest living visual writing systems in the world (Chinese) and one of the newest (emoji)? **Hanmoji** are a fun way of writing Chinese characters using emoji. We call this book *The Hanmoji Handbook* because it's filled with surprising insights emoji give us into understanding Chinese characters—and it provides ways to understand the parallel lives of these two writing systems, old and new.

We'll begin around 1000 BCE as hanzi were first being developed, and span the years up to today, exploring how language grows and changes, how it's shaped by technology, and what hanzi can teach us as we watch new languages develop. Along the way, we'll also learn a few dozen Chinese words and a bit about **linguistics**, or the study of language.

Ready to start?
走吧 (*zǒu ba/zau2 baa1*)
Let's go!

Introducing Our Intrepid Guide

Hi! I'm Jiji. In Chinese, my name is ヨヨ, or "Snout Snout," based on an ancient Chinese word. I like sniffing around books and learning new things. I'll be your guide through the world of hanmoji, sharing tips and tricks along the way.

Name	Jiji / ヨヨ
Hanmoji name	🐽 🐽
Age	✌️ Two years old (ten in human years!)
Favorite color	⬛ Boar-own
Favorite class	🀄 Chinese class!
Favorite food	🌽🥕🥬🥒
Favorite activity	🧺 Pig-nics

Here are some photos of my friends and family!

Mom's baby photo

Me and my best friend on vacation

My cousin Cerdo

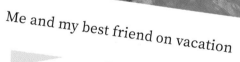

A latte-art selfie!

1
Chinese, Hanzi, and Hanmoji

Your First Hanmoji

▶ Pull up the emoji keyboard on your phone.

This is what it looks like on an Apple phone.

And here's what it looks like on an Android phone.

Can't find the keyboard? Ask someone for help!

Let's take this emoji. You would use it to say "tree," right?

What if you used two of them? That would be a few trees, right? Maybe a forest of trees? Guess what! This is how Chinese works, too!

This is the Chinese word for "wood." Kind of looks like a tree, huh?

Now, if you take two "wood" characters and squish them together, side by side . . .

you get the Chinese word for "woods" or "forest":

To remember this Chinese character, just think of it as two tree emoji bunched together in a forest.

林 = 🌲🌲

This is a hanmoji: a way of writing Chinese using emoji that makes it fun, colorful, and easy to remember.

Alphabetic versus Logographic Languages

▶ English uses an **alphabet**, a system of writing where letters or symbols represent sounds. So do Russian, Greek, and Armenian, though they each use different alphabets.

LETTERS OF THE ALPHABET IN . . .	
English	ABCDEFGHIJKLMNOPQRSTUVWXYZ
Russian	АБВГДЕЁЖЗИЙКЛМНОПРСТУФХЦЧШЩЪЫЬЭЮЯ
Greek	ΑΒΓΔΕΖΗΘΙΚΛΜΝΞΟΠΡΣΤΥΦΧΨΩ
Armenian	ԱԲԳԴԵԶԷԹԺԻԼԽԾԿՀՁՂՃՄՅՆՇՈՉՊՋՌՍՎՏՐՑՒՓՔՕՖ

The Russian and Armenian alphabets have more than thirty letters!

With an alphabetic language, you can generally guess how a word is pronounced by learning each letter and its sounds. What's more, all the words and ideas in those languages are made up using combinations of the same letters!

p   **i**   **g**

"pee"   "eye"   "jee"

Written Chinese doesn't use an alphabet. It's a logographic language, which means that it uses **logograms** (symbols or signs) to represent words. Many people assume Chinese characters are pure **pictograms**, or drawings that represent exactly what they describe. That's true for some words, like *wood,* which we talked about earlier, but it's not true for all words.

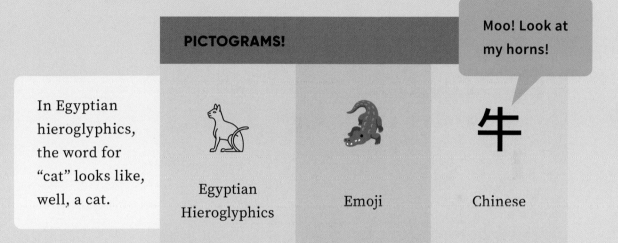

In Egyptian hieroglyphics, the word for "cat" looks like, well, a cat.

PICTOGRAMS!

Moo! Look at my horns!

Egyptian Hieroglyphics

Emoji

Chinese

DID YOU KNOW? Ancient logographic languages often depicted animals that were important to the speakers of those languages. The tools that were available shaped the way the animals were drawn. Sumerian, for example, was written using a blunt, angular reed on a clay tablet, which explains why the word for "fish" is made up of simple, bold lines. Mayan, on the other hand, was often carved and molded in stucco, which explains why the word for "snake" allows for much more detail and looks like it came out of a square mold. Just think how different that is compared with tapping on an animal emoji on your phone today!

The Chinese Zodiac

The Chinese zodiac is an astrological system that assigns people an animal based on the year they're born. Each of the twelve zodiac animals has its own personality and characteristics, and they follow a twelve-year cycle. So if you're a tiger, people born twelve years after you and twelve years before you are also tigers.

If you're a pig, like me, you're the last of the animals in the twelve-year cycle.

I'm a tiger, which means I was born three years after or nine years before a pig, and my, my, you look tasty . . .

Match These Things!

Can you match the Sumerian, Mayan, and Traditional Chinese characters below to the emoji zodiac on the facing page?

The Chinese Zodiac

A Twelve-Year Cycle

PIG · RAT · DOG · OX · CHICKEN · TIGER · MONKEY · RABBIT · GOAT · DRAGON · HORSE · SNAKE

There Is More Than One Chinese Language

▶ What language do Chinese people speak? If you said Chinese, you're right! But which Chinese is the big question. Here's the thing about spoken Chinese: it refers to many different languages—dozens, in fact—used by people in various parts of China, today and throughout history. Linguists have defined up to ten different Chinese language groups, each of which has its own subgroups. Some language groups sound as similar to each other as Spanish and Italian, but some are as different from each

Ten language groups?!

Why Are There So Many Chinese Languages?

Languages rarely have hard-and-fast boundaries, and sometimes the labels we use to describe a language aren't exact. Take English, for example. Do you say "mom," "mum," "mama," or "mother"? These all mean the same thing, but you might use a different word or have a different accent if you learned your English in the United States instead of in, say, Trinidad or England.

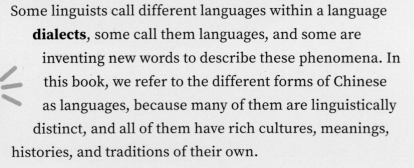 Some linguists call different languages within a language **dialects**, some call them languages, and some are inventing new words to describe these phenomena. In this book, we refer to the different forms of Chinese as languages, because many of them are linguistically distinct, and all of them have rich cultures, meanings, histories, and traditions of their own.

other as German and Swahili, which are **mutually unintelligible**, or unable to be understood between speakers. People speaking Cantonese, for example, can't understand people speaking Shanghainese, and vice versa.

In this book, the pronunciations appear in Mandarin Chinese—the main language in mainland China and Taiwan, and one of the most common languages in Singapore. We also include Cantonese—the main language in Hong Kong and Macau, which is also spoken in mainland China's Southeast and in many Chinatowns around the world.

Contemporary Chinese Uses Romanization and More Than One Chinese Writing System

Romanization is the process of expressing a writing system using the Roman (or Latin) alphabet. There are several forms of romanization for the many Chinese languages, and sometimes multiple romanizations for one Chinese language. Mandarin, for example, has two main ones: Wade-Giles and Pinyin.

While there may be many forms of spoken Chinese, the two most widely used written ones are Traditional and Simplified. This is why the written language is so handy: people who speak different forms of Chinese can usually understand the same words written down. Written Chinese is much more unified than spoken Chinese because Emperor Qin introduced a standardized script for scholars, poets, and government bureaucrats to communicate with one another across all of China.

Traditional characters are most commonly used in Taiwan, Hong Kong, and Macau. These characters have been used for hundreds of years and have barely changed since the fifth century. Simplified characters were developed in the 1940s, '50s, and '60s. They're used primarily in mainland China, Singapore, and Malaysia, and as the name implies, they're simpler to write and remember.

But how do dozens of spoken languages share writing systems? People simply write the same thing but pronounce it differently.

The Many Pigs of China

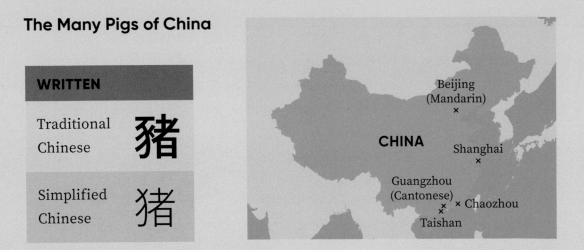

WRITTEN	
Traditional Chinese	豬
Simplified Chinese	猪

SPOKEN		
Chinese Language	**Pronunciation**	**Place(s) of Origin**
Mandarin	*zhū*	Northern China
Cantonese	*zyu1*	Guangdong Province
Teochew	*de1*	Chaoshan/Chaozhou
Taishanese	*dzi33*	Taishan
Shanghainese	*tsy1*	Shanghai

What's up with the numbers and that line above the *u* in *zhū*? Some Chinese romanization systems include numbers or marks to indicate tones, or pitches, used to pronounce the words. We'll talk more about tones in a few pages.

In case you're having trouble deciding which type of spoken and written Chinese to learn, we made a handy chart to help you figure that out:

	Mandarin	**Cantonese**
Traditional Chinese	You're into Taiwan's culture and music, and you might have family ties there. You like learning about language history and want to read classical Chinese texts.	You like Hong Kong movies and pop culture. You might want to visit or live there one day and may have some family ties there and/or in another part of Guangdong Province.
Simplified Chinese	You're interested in the art, culture, and news coming out of mainland China. You want to visit or work there one day and/or have family ties there.	You have family ties to Guangdong Province, might want to live in China, and are not that interested in Hong Kong culture.

If you have family or friends who speak Chinese, ask them for their opinion.

How Chinese Characters Are Shown in This Book

The Traditional Chinese character appears first in bold, followed by the Simplified Chinese character. If the Traditional and Simplified Chinese characters are the same, we show the character only once.

豬
猪

zhū

zyu1

pig

The English definition appears beside the Chinese characters.

The pronunciation is listed first in Mandarin (Pinyin), then in Cantonese (Jyutping).

The Chinese Language Is Totally Tonal

mā 媽 妈 mother

má 麻 麻 hemp

mǎ 馬 马 horse

mà 罵 骂 scold

▶ While Chinese languages can vary widely when spoken, one thing they have in common is that they're all **tonal**. That means that they use pitch in individual spoken words (similar to the way our voices get higher at the end of a question to indicate that it's a question). When you change the tone of a word, you change its meaning.

Mandarin has four tones. The first tone is a level tone, as when calmly saying "Yeah" in English. The second tone rises, like when you're asking a question in English: "What?" The third tone falls and then rises, almost like you're asking a question and it's being stretched: "Cooool?" The fourth tone drops sharply, like when you're scolding someone: "No!"

In this book, we represent Mandarin's tones with **diacritical marks**, which appear above vowels to indicate their pronunciation. These marks look like the tones:

ā sounds level

á rises

ǎ dips and rises back up

à drops straight down

mā mà mǎ
Mother scolds
the horse.

In this book, we use **Pinyin**, a pronunciation system for Mandarin standardized in the 1950s in mainland China that uses letters from the English alphabet along with the tone marks above.

Cantonese has six or nine tones, depending on which romanization system you use. We will be using the **Jyutping** system, which was developed by the Linguistic Society of Hong Kong in 1993 and also uses letters from the English alphabet.

It has six tones:

saam1	wun2	bun3	ngau4	naam5	min6
三	碗	半	牛	腩	麵
三	碗	半	牛	腩	面
three	bowl	and a half	beef	brisket	noodles

These six Cantonese tones are a little bit harder to tell apart than their counterparts in Mandarin. They are often called:

high level *or* high falling	mid rising	mid level	low falling	low rising	low level

How to Use Pinyin and Jyutping

▶ On the previous pages, we showed how tones are represented in the Mandarin Pinyin and Cantonese Jyutping pronunciation systems. You probably noticed that they both use letters from the English alphabet. But here's the thing: many of the English letters in Pinyin and Jyutping aren't pronounced exactly the way they are in English.

Here is a beginner's guide to what the letters are supposed to sound like. Don't worry about memorizing everything right now—just refer back to this section as you make your way through the book. For further study, we recommend listening to some language-learning podcasts or taking a class with fluent Chinese speakers. There's really no substitute for practicing with real people when it comes to language learning.

> Did you know the *pin* in *Pinyin* means "pieced together" and the *yin* means "sound"?

PINYIN

c sounds like the *ts* in *its*

i sounds like the *ee* in *see*

q sounds like the *ch* in *chips*

r sounds like an elongated *r* in *rrribbit*

ü sounds like the *yu* in *yule*

x sounds like *sh* as in *shh, no talking in the library*

z sounds like the buzzy *ds* in *lids* and *woods*

zh sounds like the *s* in *treasure*

拼音
pīnyīn

JYUTPING

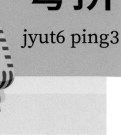

粤拼

jyut6 ping3

Letters at the start of words

c sounds like *tsh*

j sounds like the *y* in *yes*

n sounds like an *l*

ng sounds like the *n* in *ink*

z sounds like a *j* with a *buzz*

Vowels in the middle and at the end are often stretched out

a sounds like the *u* in *cup*

aa sounds like the *a* in *father*

ai sounds like the *i* in *hi*

i sounds like *ee*

o sounds like the *o* in *so*

u sounds like the *oo* in *moon*

Letters at the end of words

an ending *k* is short and guttural

an ending *p* is short and clipped

Another Way to Remember the Six Jyutping Tones

The six tones can also be roughly mapped to the often-sung "do-re-mi-fa-sol" scale that many of us learn in music class. The mapping below is a handy shortcut for understanding how the tones sound relative to one another and why the tones are classified as high/mid/low.

these two tones slide up

Similar to how Pinyin means "pieced together" and "sound," *Jyutping* means "pieced together" and a shorthand for "Cantonese."

Tonal Trivia

 DID YOU KNOW? Tonal languages might seem tough at first, but they're actually quite common. Approximately 70 percent of all languages are tonal. Tones are most used in East Asia, Southeast Asia, and sub-Saharan Africa and in Indigenous languages in Mexico.

WHICH OF THESE ARE TONAL LANGUAGES?

English	Korean	Mandarin
Navajo	Punjabi	Russian
Spanish	Thai	Zulu

Here's a hint: There are five.

Answer: Mandarin, Navajo, Punjabi, Thai, and Zulu are tonal.

But There's a Catch!

You can also have different Chinese characters with different meanings but with the same sound (including tone)!

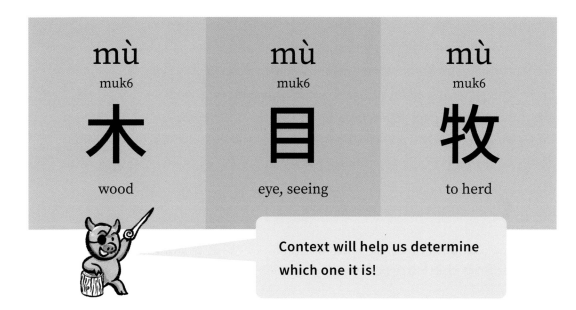

Really, though, English does the same thing sometimes:

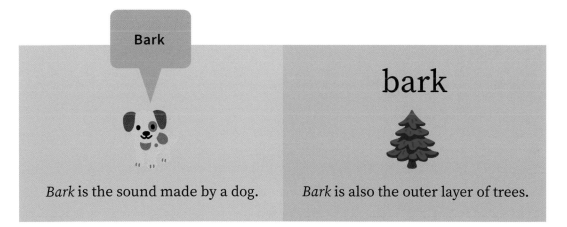

Same sound, different meanings.

How Chinese Characters Work

▶ Remember, Chinese characters are considered logograms, which means that each character usually represents a single word. Unlike a word in an alphabetic language, a logogram doesn't spell out a pronunciation. It just shows you what the word is.

People generally agree that you need to know about four thousand Chinese characters in order to read well. But does that mean you need to memorize that many unique logograms? Not exactly. Luckily, Chinese characters reuse a lot of the same building blocks, which makes the language that much easier to learn and remember.

Four thousand things to remember!

Introducing the Radical

These reusable building blocks are called **radicals**. They can represent things or ideas or help you with pronunciation. Radicals are often used for organizing and classifying Chinese characters. The good news is that there are only about 217 radicals, which are used and reused across thousands of characters. The bad news is that while some characters are made up of just radicals, others are unique logograms that don't use any radicals or are a mix of radicals and unique logograms.

 DID YOU KNOW? The word *radical* and the word *radish* both come from the Latin word for "root"! **Etymology** is the study of words and their origins, and it's just as fun in English as it is in Chinese.

The Double Life of a Radical Chinese Character

Many Chinese characters can also be used as radicals. For example, 羊 (*yáng/joeng4*) is the character for a goat or sheep, but it's a sheep-ish radical, too. The character for water, 水 (*shuǐ/seoi2*), is also a radical. As you can imagine, there are many water-related Chinese characters that require this aqueous radical.

But some radicals, like "water," lead a double life. They actually appear under two different guises as building blocks in Chinese characters:

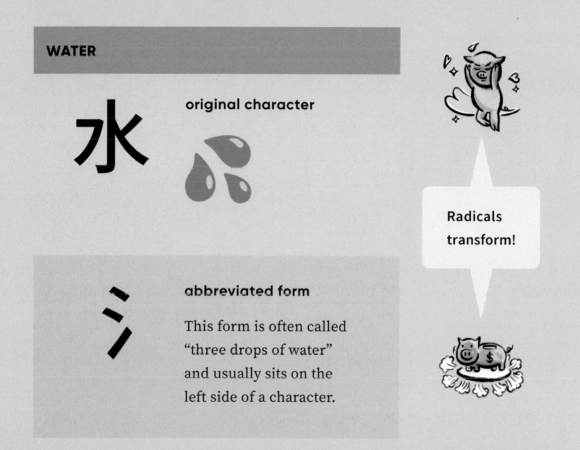

WATER

original character

abbreviated form

This form is often called "three drops of water" and usually sits on the left side of a character.

Radicals transform!

The goat/sheep radical, however, does not lead such an exciting life. It may appear a bit stretched or squashed in a Chinese character, but it doesn't have an alternative form.

Let's dive into an example using these two radicals:

水 氵 water
shuǐ
soei2

羊 sheep
yáng
joeng4

Put them together, and the character becomes . . . "ocean."

洋 ocean
yáng
joeng4

While it's impossible to know from the character alone that 洋 (*yáng/joeng4*) stands for "ocean," the two radicals inside it can give us hints about what the character means and how to say it.

洋

氵

Hint 1: Meaning

The **semantic radical** helps you understand what the word is about. In this case, that's water.

羊

Hint 2: Pronunciation

The **phonetic radical** helps you understand how to pronounce the word. In this case, that's *yang*. Sheep have nothing to do with the ocean, but they help us pronounce this word!

So to learn this character, you still have to memorize it, but there are clues to help you along the way.

Characters made up of radicals are not always so easy to decipher, though. Take "fresh," for example:

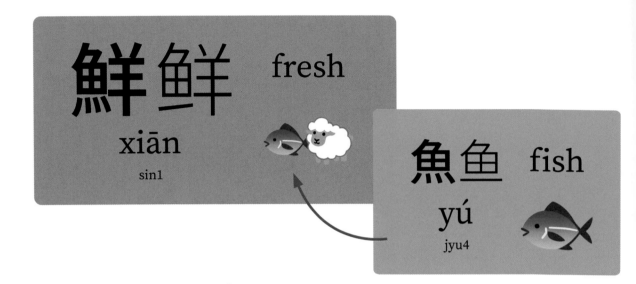

The left half is "fish." The right half is "sheep" (羊 *yáng/joeng4*). The idea that both fish and lamb are best eaten when fresh makes sense for the semantics, or meaning. But 鮮/鲜 *xiān/sin1* ("fresh") sounds like neither 魚 *yú/jyu4* ("fish") nor 羊 *yáng/joeng4* ("sheep"). You'll just have to memorize that one! Or take:

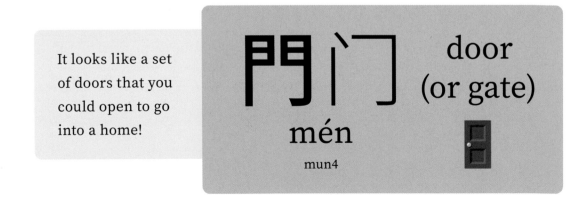

It looks like a set of doors that you could open to go into a home!

If you add a mouth to a door or gate:

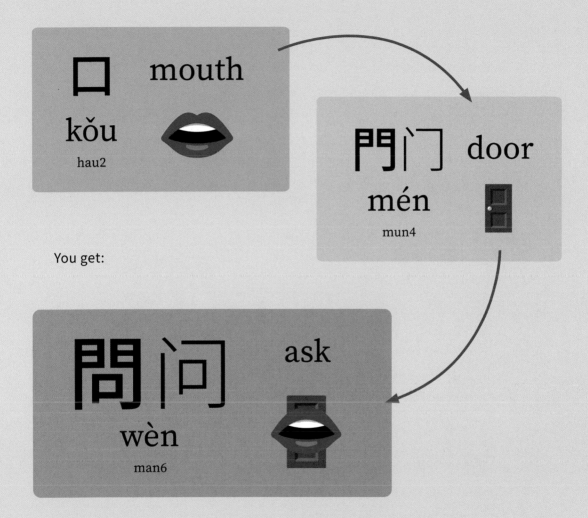

You get:

It's like someone's calling through the gate. Here, we're getting a lot of semantic cues, but 門/门 *mén/mun4* ("door" or "gate") and 問/问 *wèn/man6* ("ask") don't sound exactly alike, although they do rhyme.

Why Hanmoji?

▶ Imagine if you could have as much fun learning Chinese characters (hanzi) as you do when you're learning emoji. That's what hanmoji are all about—the place where emoji and hanzi meet. Studying hanmoji also gives us insight into the history of written languages as we think about the future of how we talk online.

Chinese characters

漢字
汉字
hànzì
hon3 zi6

Have you ever used this emoji to mean that you're looking at something?

Or this to say you agree with someone?

You're not *literally* saying "eyeballs" or "100." These are examples of **figurative** uses of language, where words and phrases create vivid pictures and take on new meanings in different contexts. This is part of how language evolves and changes. It's how we get an expression like 馬上/马上 (*mǎshàng/maa5seong6*), or "on a horse." Before cars and trains, riding horses was the fastest way for people to get from one place to another. Thus, today, saying "on a horse" in Chinese means "right away."

Studying the Chinese language isn't always easy, but by learning more about its history and cultural context, and breaking it down to see what makes characters work, you can understand the stories of how people write, think, and express thoughts using Chinese. And the best part is that it requires the same creativity and imagination as typing out a funny emoji sequence to a friend.

So shall we get started? Get on a 馬/马 (*mǎ/maa5*) and turn the page!

Hold on. What is a hanmoji again?

Hanmoji
noun

1. a way of writing Chinese characters and radicals using emoji

2. a handy way to learn Chinese characters

2
The Five Elements

Introducing the
Five Chinese Elements

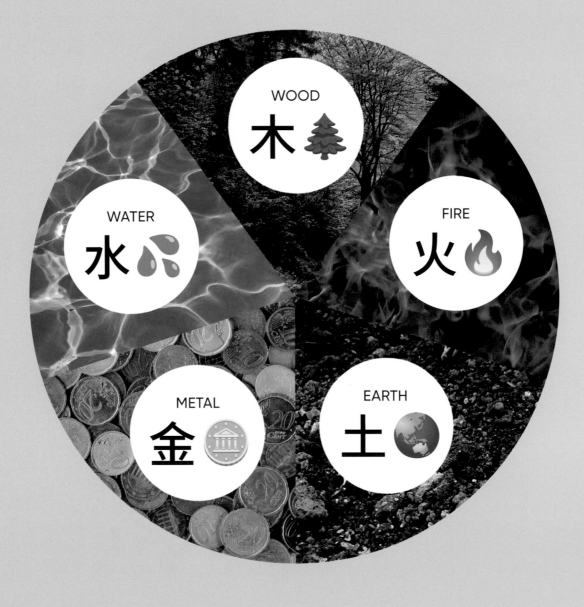

WOOD
木🌲

WATER
水💦

FIRE
火🔥

METAL
金🏛️

EARTH
土🌏

▶ **Daoism** is a philosophical tradition from ancient China that focuses on living in harmony with the **Dao**, or Way, of the universe. In Daoism, there are five elements, known as the **wuxing** (五行 *wǔxíng/ng5hang4*). These elements inform everything from astrology to architecture, medicine to music, and even tea, martial arts, and poetry.

Instead of being static, these elements are processes that are constantly flowing and changing. That's why the word *wuxing* includes *xing* (行 *xíng/hang4*), which means "movement"! Elements can even produce one another; for example, wood produces fire by serving as fuel.

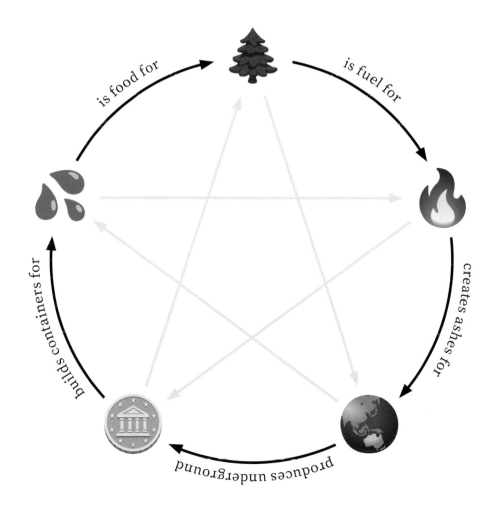

is food for

is fuel for

creates ashes for

produces underground

builds containers for

Ever use water to put out a fire? Or watch how the roots of a tree pop out from the ground? The elements don't just provide fuel for one another. They can also overcome one another. Here are the overcoming cycles in the wuxing system:

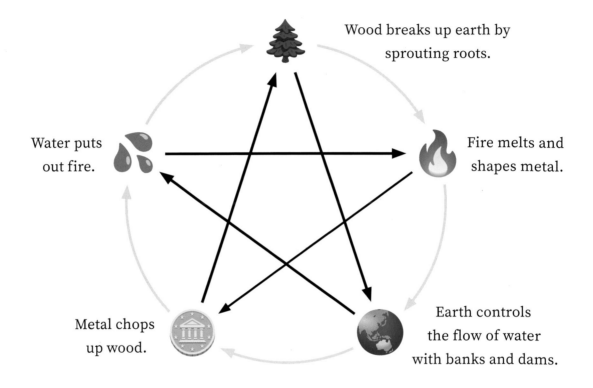

Wood breaks up earth by sprouting roots.

Fire melts and shapes metal.

Water puts out fire.

Earth controls the flow of water with banks and dams.

Metal chops up wood.

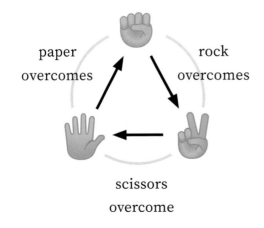

paper overcomes

rock overcomes

scissors overcome

Have you ever played rock, paper, scissors? If so, you're playing a game of overcoming cycles—rock overcomes scissors, scissors overcome paper, and paper overcomes rock. Games like this have been played around the world for thousands of years!

Wind and Water

Feng shui is a traditional set of Chinese principles for living harmoniously with the environment, whether in your home or out in nature. The term literally means "wind and water," and the concept is associated with finding balance among the five elements. For feng shui practitioners, balancing the elements is key to a happy home with good **qi**, or energy.

In feng shui, the color green represents wood energy, which is growing and expansive. Red represents fire, with passion and illumination. A room with wood and fire energy can be a good space for creative work. If you find you're frequently anxious, the yellow of earth can help calm and soothe you. The whites and grays of metal offer opportunities to find beauty, and black objects stand in for water, encouraging flowing energy.

Try arranging these elements in a room, using either colors or actual materials (like a wooden bookshelf with metal decor) and see how you feel.

風水
风水
fēngshuǐ
fung1 seoi2

Let's Learn Some New Words!

木 wood

mù

muk6

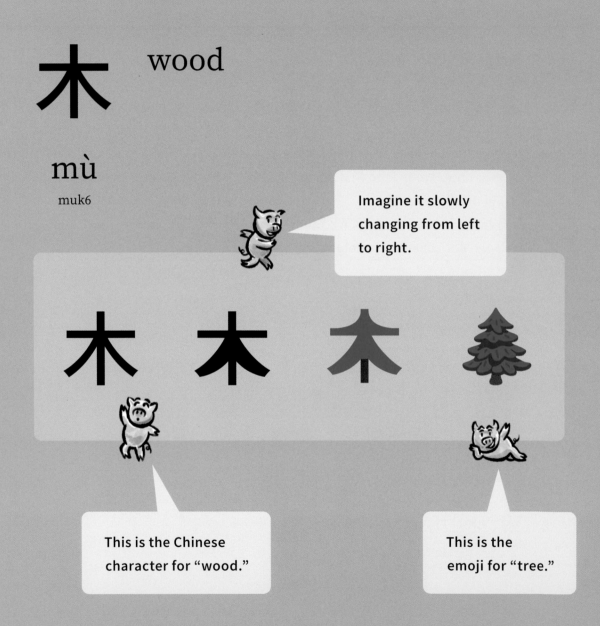

Imagine it slowly changing from left to right.

This is the Chinese character for "wood."

This is the emoji for "tree."

火 fire

huǒ

fo2

Imagine the smoldering fire, its flames licking upward.

This is fine.

水

water

shuǐ

seoi2

Long ago, Chinese was written using ink brushes (and often still is).

水　水

This character is made up of three brushstrokes, each one a drop of water.

土 earth, soil

tǔ
tou2

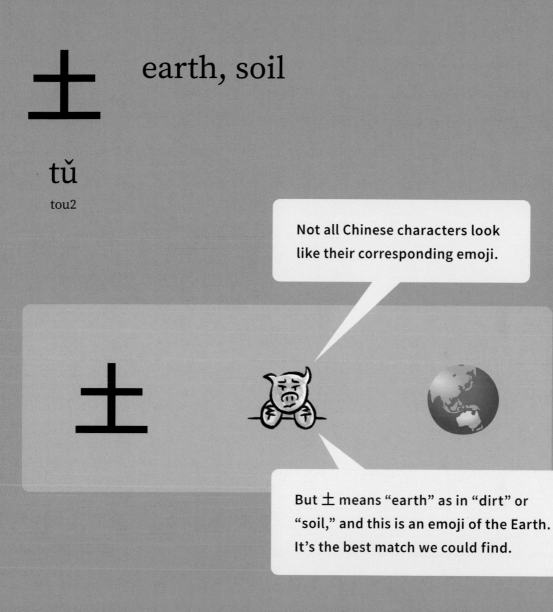

Not all Chinese characters look like their corresponding emoji.

But 土 means "earth" as in "dirt" or "soil," and this is an emoji of the Earth. It's the best match we could find.

The character for "earth" is a bit more abstract. It comes from a pictogram of a little lump of clay on top of a potter's wheel.

Over time, it came to look like this character, which represents the earth or ground—where potters get their clay.

metal, gold

jīn

gam1

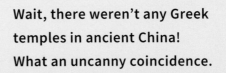

Wait, there weren't any Greek temples in ancient China! What an uncanny coincidence.

Chinese characters can be tricky! The character for metal or gold might look like a little house or building, but it's a combination of two different parts. The word for "metal" is a good example of a **phonosemantic character**—a character that includes both a phonetic (sound) radical and a semantic (meaning) radical. But in this case, the radicals are ancient forms that are no longer used in Chinese today.

Let's break the character down, starting with the bottom part:

This is a variant of the character for "king" (王 *wáng/wong4*). Is it because kings like gold? Actually, it's because the character 王 used to have a thicker bottom and looked like an upside-down ax, and this battle ax represented the power worthy of a king. In this case, though, the character is used to refer to the metallic nature of the ax.

Now take a look at the top part:

This indicates the sound of the word, which in this case is derived from 今 (*jīn/gam1*). You'll see other words that sound like *jīn/gam1*, too.

Combining the Elements

▶ The Chinese characters for the five elements are also radicals in their own right and can be combined with themselves or one another to form other characters. Let's start with a fiery example:

火 **fire**

huǒ

fo2

炎 **inflammation**

yán

jim4

焱 **flames**

yàn

jim6

I'm all fired up!

One fire character is easy: it means fire. Imagine the character as a lit match.

When two fires meet, things start getting hot—inflamed, even.

Gather three bits of fire closely, and we get flames! Imagine three burning logs coming together.

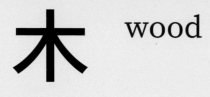 wood

mù

muk6

林 forest, grove

lín

lam4

The woods are lovely, dark and deep, but I have hanmoji to keep.

森 full of trees or dark and gloomy

sēn

sam1

The character on the left usually means "wood" but can also mean "tree."

Two trees make a forest, or *lin*. Lin also happens to be a popular last name. Think of basketball star Jeremy Lin dribbling a ball along a forest path.

Three trees can mean "full of trees" or "dark and gloomy," as in a dense forest.

淡

dàn

daam6

Let's turn this character into its hanmoji:

It helps to break apart the character into its core elements first: three drops 氵 of water and two 火, or flames.

 淡

 氵火火

Make a mental image of what's happening. Here's one way of envisioning it:

Hint: What happens to a fire when water is sprayed on it?

Answer: The fire becomes weaker. So this whole character, made of two flames and some water, means "mild," "faint," or "weak."

鈥
鈥
huǒ
fo2

holmium (a rare metal)

This character refers to **holmium**, a rare-earth mineral that was discovered in 1878. Do you recognize its two parts?

The first part, 金 (*jīn/gam1*), "metal," is semantic: it carries some of the character's meaning (in the simplified Chinese radical, 金 is written as 钅, which saves three strokes). The second part, 火 (*huǒ/fo2*), "fire," is phonetic, since the Mandarin pronunciation, *huǒ*, sounds like the beginning of *holmium*. (The name *holmium* comes from Holmia, the Latin name for Stockholm, which is the hometown of one of the scientists who discovered the element.) The second part ("fire") is also semantic, because holmium burns easily.

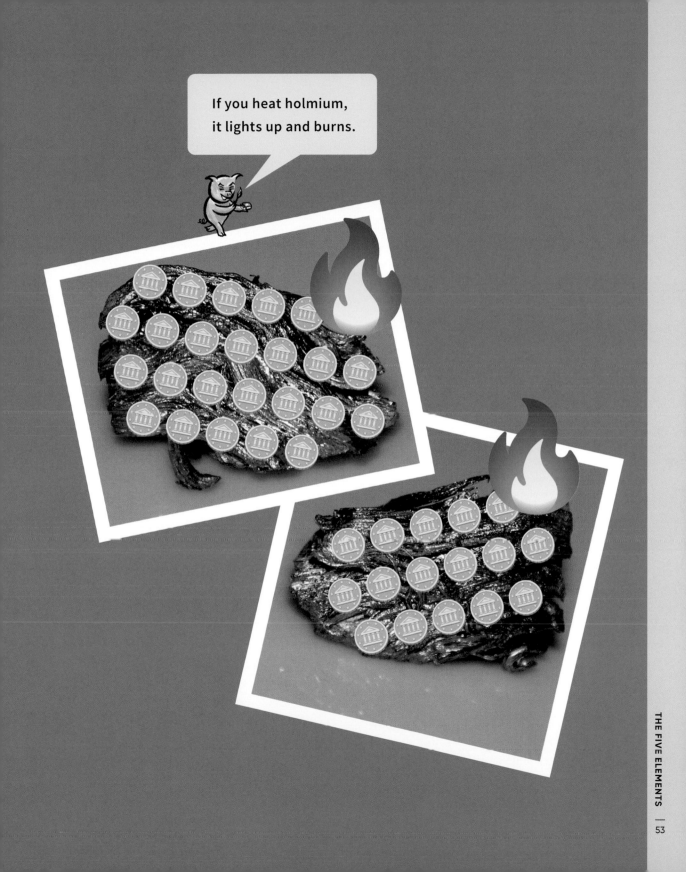

焚

burn

fén

fan4

Set a fire (火 *huǒ/fo2*) under two pieces of wood (木 *mù/muk6*), and what happens? They burn up! This word tends to be used for big fires, like forest fires.

焚香 (***fénxiāng/fan4hoeng1***) refers to burning incense.

Invent Your Own Hanmoji!

▶ Take out a blank sheet of paper. Then, using emoji of the five elements, make up your own hanmoji characters! How else might fire and water be combined? What about earth and metal? And what does it mean when you put them together?

> Magic elements, I call on you . . . COMBINE!

REAL-LIFE EXAMPLES

It might help to first think about how you could arrange your emoji by copying these templates:

How would you use these characters in a text message to your friends?

Is What You've Drawn a Real Chinese Character? Only One Way to Find Out . . .

Next to your hanmoji drawings or on a new piece of paper, translate your invention into Chinese.

Now here's the fun part! But it's not going to be easy, so you might want to get someone to help you.

Go on your computer and search for a Chinese dictionary. You can use www.mdbg.net or Google Translate. At mdbg.net, look for the brush or pencil icon. In Google Translate, look for the gray icon on the bottom right corner of the box where you input text. Click it.

That should open up a box for you to enter your newly invented Chinese character. Try drawing it in and see if it matches any existing Chinese characters. Drawing on a computer is tricky, so it might take a few tries. There's a higher chance that what you've drawn is not a Chinese character, but that doesn't mean there aren't new Chinese characters to be invented! Language is always evolving and changing, and it's fun to play with words and writing to learn more about how language works.

EMOJI-TO-CHINESE LOOKUP TABLE

木

火

土

金

水

3

How Languages Evolve

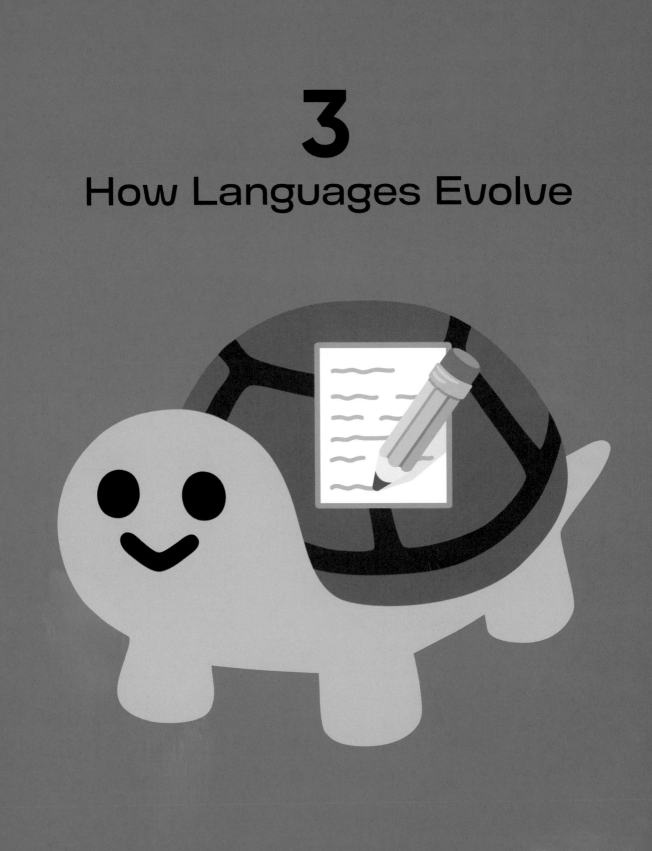

From Bones to Brushes: A Brief History of Hanzi

▶ The earliest Chinese writing can be found inside tortoise shells! More than four thousand years ago, during the Shang dynasty, oracle bones captured inscriptions of **divination** proceedings. Divination is the practice of trying to figure out the future, and the Shang emperor tried to speak to ancestors and deities for guidance about government affairs. These findings about the future were captured on the bones of tortoises, oxen, and other animals.

When Emperor Qin unified what we now know as China in 221 BCE, one of his first priorities was to create a standard written language across the lands he had just conquered. By 206 BCE, the Qin dynasty had succeeded in establishing an official script. Because writing was done with brushes, Chinese characters took on curved strokes in addition to the hard angles more commonly used in the days of inscribing onto animal bones.

By the time of the Southern and Northern dynasties (420–589 CE), Chinese script had taken on basic forms that continue today, more than 1,500 years later!

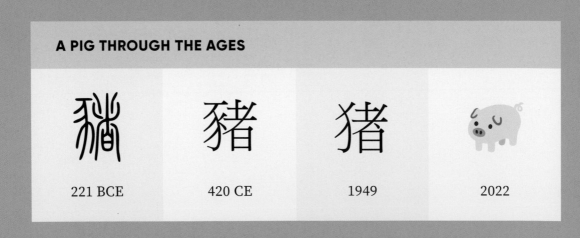

A PIG THROUGH THE AGES

| 221 BCE | 420 CE | 1949 | 2022 |

Have you ever noticed how your handwriting looks different when you write with a pen on paper versus when you write on a chalkboard? The tools we use to write affect how our words appear. The Chinese language has evolved over time, not just because it was created so long ago but also because people have been using different tools through the ages.

QIN DYNASTY

221–207 BCE
14 years

Emperor Qin
Shi Huang
(ruled 221–210 BCE)

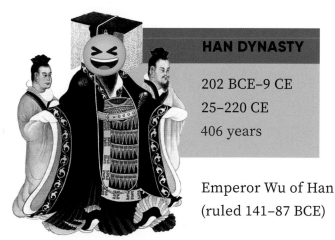

HAN DYNASTY

202 BCE–9 CE
25–220 CE
406 years

Emperor Wu of Han
(ruled 141–87 BCE)

But Why Are Chinese Characters—Hanzi—Named after the Han Dynasty?

It's true that Emperor Qin might deserve credit for standardizing written Chinese. But unfortunately for him, the Qin dynasty lasted only fifteen years. In comparison, the Han dynasty, which followed, lasted 406 years and is generally considered the first great dynastic era in China. So that's why Chinese characters are called hanzi, and the most common ethnic group in China is called **hanren** (漢人/汉人 *hànrén/ hon3jan4*), or the Han people.

The Creation of Simplified Chinese

The Republic of China formed in 1912 after the fall of the Qing dynasty, during a time of great turmoil not just in China but also around the world. When a new national government forms, there are often many changes, including to language. One of the new Republican government's major tasks was to figure out a common language for the country's many citizens. Even with one official script, there were still many forms of spoken Chinese, and the new technologies of the day allowed more people to hear one another through the radio and, eventually, film and television.

Some people advocated for maintaining the traditional script. Others thought it would be better to simplify the characters, making them easier to remember and write, which would help raise literacy rates (at the time, most of the population couldn't read or write). This debate continued for many years—through a period of civil war and World War II.

Traditional Chinese	Simplified Chinese
繁體中文	簡體中文
繁体中文	简体中文
fántǐ zhōngwén	jiǎntǐ zhōngwén
faan4 tai2 zung1 man4	gaan2 tai2 zung1 man4

When you choose Chinese on a website, these are usually the two options that show up!

In 1949, the People's Republic of China established the National Conference on Script Reform to figure out what to do with all the characters. Some people even argued for getting rid of Chinese characters completely, but Mao Zedong, the first chairman of the People's Republic of China, felt it would be too disruptive. Although countries like Korea and Vietnam, which previously used Chinese characters, had moved on to alphabetic systems, China ultimately went forward with simplified characters, continuing in the logographic tradition.

As the debate raged on, the Committee for Reforming the Chinese Written Language was established to create new standards, borrowing from forms with fewer brushstrokes that people were already using in informal settings. And so Simplified Chinese was born, and it's still used today throughout mainland China, Malaysia, and Singapore. But if you visit an old temple or other historic sites, you might see some Traditional Chinese.

In Taiwan, Hong Kong, Macau, and the Philippines, people use Traditional Chinese characters in signs, newspapers, TV shows, and books. They're also used in Korea and parts of Thailand, where people don't speak Chinese but use Chinese characters in a limited way to express certain words. They're used in Japanese as well.

A Living Tradition

If you go to mainland China today, it's still easy to find Traditional Chinese characters throughout historic sites like temples, palaces, and gardens. But even within these places, the signs and notices are all written in Simplified Chinese.

From Hanzi to Hanmoji:
A Millennia-Long Evolution

ORACLE BONE INSCRIPTIONS	SMALL SEAL SCRIPT	CLERICAL SCRIPT	REGULAR SCRIPT/ TRADITIONAL CHINESE
1600–1046 BCE	221–206 BCE	206 BCE–220 CE	420–589 CE

This character hadn't been invented here yet!

SIMPLIFIED CHINESE	HANMOJI
1949 CE	2022 CE

Many Simplified and Traditional Chinese Characters Are the Same!

Not every Chinese character has different Simplified and Traditional forms. One good example is 中, "middle" (*zhōng/zung1*); another is 人, "person" (*rén/jan4*). Even some words that might seem more complex, like 海, "sea" (*hǎi/hoi2*), and 清, "clear" (*qīng/ceng1*), remain the same in both forms.

HOW LANGUAGES EVOLVE

65

A Brief History of Emoji

1999
NTT DoCoMo

2002
au by KDDI

2004
Softbank

2008
Apple iOS

2013
Samsung

2015
HTC

2017
Google
Android

2019
Microsoft
Windows

▶ The emoji we know and love today started in Japan. Japanese people had been adding small images to their mobile-phone text messages since the late 1990s, but many of them were just in black and white. Then designer Shigetaka Kurita created colorful images for a Japanese phone company called NTT DoCoMo. They were called "e-mo-ji," which means "picture character" in Japanese.

Kurita drew each of the original emoji on a twelve-by-twelve-pixel grid. He made more than 170 drawings, including a heart, a cat (pictured at the upper left), a shoe, a snowman, a purse, a sun, and a cloud. These emoji were released in 1999 by NTT DoCoMo, and they quickly became popular among mobile-phone users in Japan.

Soon, Japanese phone companies all added colorful picture characters to their new phones, but there was one catch—each company created a different set of pictures. The problem was similar to the one that vexed Emperor Qin: mismatched emoji meant people couldn't always communicate with one another if they weren't carrying phones from the same company.

In 2002, if a friend sent you this angry-face emoji . . .

 and you had an NTT DoCoMo phone, you saw an impish pout.

 But if you had a SoftBank phone, you saw a very angry face.

In the 2000s, Japanese people began sending email on their mobile phones, which meant the messages needed to be readable on all kinds of phones *and* computers. This heightened the need for a global, shared system of emoji.

In 2007, companies asked for help from the Unicode Consortium, a nonprofit organization that helps create shared systems for writing on all kinds of devices, including computers and telephones. This made sense because emoji were a new form of written communication.

It took three years for Unicode to create the first shared emoji system. They combined images from all the different Japanese telephone companies and in 2010 released the first set with more than seven hundred emoji, creating a standardized, shared system of writing and communicating.

Today, the members of the Unicode Consortium continue to decide which new emoji to add each year. Many of the ideas for emoji come from people around the world, including children and teenagers!

Wait . . . What Makes an Emoji an Emoji?

▶ Emoji are little color pictures that can be sent like text by phones and computers. They express an emotion or gesture or act as a substitute for a word or phrase. While you may see a colorful image, a computer sees a block of text.

WHAT WE SEE	WHAT A COMPUTER SEES
🐕	U+1F415
DOG	U+0044 U+004F U+0047
狗	U+72D7

The text a computer sees is called a **code point**, and it tells a computer what to display, whether it's a number, letter, or emoji! To a computer, these code points are all one block of text.

Because emoji are sent as simple codes from computer to computer, each system renders (or draws) the same emoji using its own illustration style, based on guidelines from the Unicode Consortium's Emoji Subcommittee. As you'll see, there's still some variation.

Presenting . . . the Many Emoji Pups Made by Global Technology Companies!

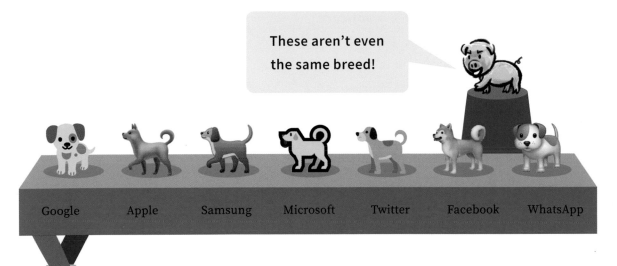

These aren't even the same breed!

| Google | Apple | Samsung | Microsoft | Twitter | Facebook | WhatsApp |

In this book, we use Google's emoji because they are part of the larger Noto font project, which is a free font system for the world's languages.

WHAT WE TYPE	WHAT WE MEAN
🐶	dog
🤔	gesture of uncertainty
🖤	heart or gesture of affection or enthusiasm

Emoji are not the only visual language people have used to express themselves on computers. Perhaps you have seen ;-) or B-) or :-P. These are called **emoticons**, and they are black-and-white pictures created with punctuation and letters, usually in the form of faces. Emoticons were most popular in the 1990s and 2000s, before emoji arrived on the scene.

Kaomoji are a kind of emoticon that use Japanese characters to create expressive illustrations, typically in the form of faces, animals, or little humans doing things. Instead of being sideways, they're right side up.

Now we also have **stickers**, which are little images or animated GIFs that people can send to one another on messaging apps. Unlike emoji and emoticons, most of the time stickers can only be sent between people using the same app.

:)   :P   :{

;-)   B-)   :'-(

(* ^ ω ^)

(づ ●‿●)づ

(ヽ °-°)ヽ ┳━┳ (ノ °□°)ノ ━━━

These stickers are from LINE, a messaging app popular in East Asia.

A common problem with visual communication is that visual writing enables flexible expression, but without standards, it's hard for people to communicate with one another on a large scale.

Emoji are relatively new. They are less than thirty years old, and they were invented to make colorful visual expression possible on mobile phones, which at the time only contained black-and-white text. Today, phones can display multi-media images, but we hope emoji are here to stay for a long time.

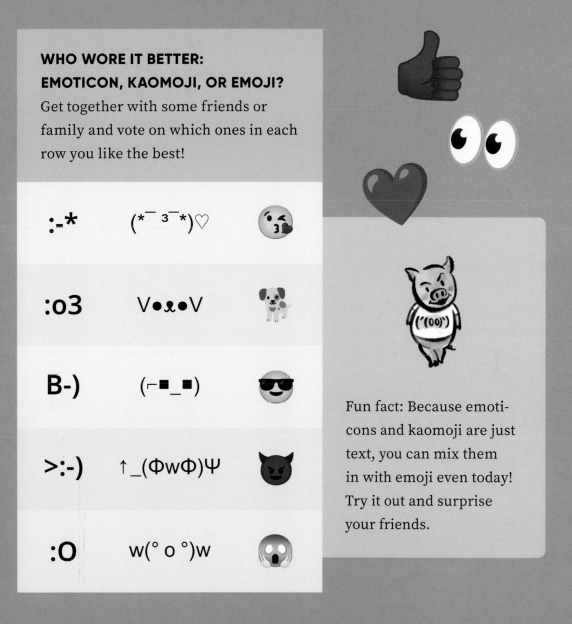

WHO WORE IT BETTER: EMOTICON, KAOMOJI, OR EMOJI?

Get together with some friends or family and vote on which ones in each row you like the best!

:-*	(*¯ ³¯*)♡	
:o3	V●ﻌ●V	
B-)	(˓■_■)	
>:-)	↑_(ΦwΦ)Ψ	
:O	w(° o °)w	

Fun fact: Because emoticons and kaomoji are just text, you can mix them in with emoji even today! Try it out and surprise your friends.

How Hanzi and Emoji Took Shape

▶ The look of a visual language depends on what's being used to write it. Earlier in this book, we learned that Sumerian has hard angles because it was written on clay using a blunt reed, while Mayan allowed for complex details and shapes because it was intricately carved and molded.

Chinese characters have mostly been written with ink brushes, enabling a form of calligraphy with many curves and flourishes. But Chinese characters also contain traces of their past. Before they were written with brush pens, words were carved into small areas of bone, jade, and bronze. So as in Sumerian, the lines were clear and sharp. This could explain why rigid, straight lines remain popular in characters even as the written language has evolved.

Emoji are no different. Our phone and computer screens have become so advanced that they can show drawings and photographs dense with color and detail. A single emoji can now fit a group of four people, each with a different hairstyle. But emoji have also inherited traces from the past, when screens were not able to display such rich images. This explains why some animal emoji are still rendered as cartoonish faces, even though most of the new animal emoji are drawn in their full-bodied splendor.

A bear in 2000 on a SoftBank phone

A bear on an Android phone twenty years later

Even though hanzi and emoji were created thousands of years apart, their historical trajectories follow similar paths.

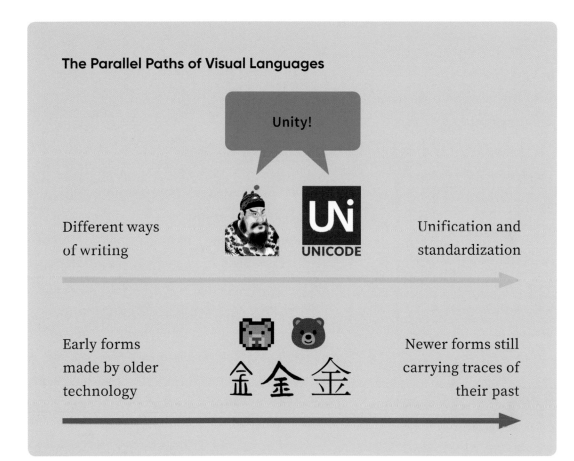

The Parallel Paths of Visual Languages

Unity!

UNICODE

Different ways of writing

Unification and standardization

Early forms made by older technology

Newer forms still carrying traces of their past

In both cases, the trend has been to make the words easier to read for more people, whether that's by agreeing on a single form or by using better technology to make characters more distinct and recognizable. But remember, unification and standardization also bear a cost: only one form wins out, so the others—our possible alternate futures—are often left behind or erased. Amid all of this, hanzi and emoji carry their histories with them—just look carefully.

Draw Your Own 1999-Style Animal Emoji

▶ What can you draw with just 144 pixels? A lot, it turns out! Follow the instructions below to practice drawing your favorite animal with just a few color pixels at your disposal.

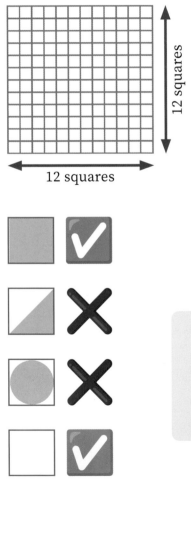

Instructions

First, set up your page. Draw a square grid that's twelve squares across and down. It can be as big as you want, as long as all the squares are the same size! You can even use graph paper if you have some around the house.

Now, here are the rules for this drawing. You can color any of the squares, but each square must either be fully filled in with one color or not be filled in at all. This kind of grid-based art is sometimes called "pixel art."

Here's a self-portrait I made using pixel art!

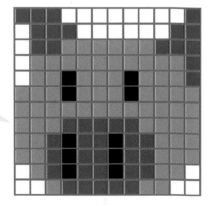

So What Exactly Is a Pixel?

A **pixel** is a tiny square dot on your
screen that can show a color. A small
smartphone screen can have more
than a million pixels, allowing you to
see lots of rich colors for videos and
photos.

Your picture is twelve pixels tall
and twelve pixels wide. That's 144
pixels, or less than 1 percent of a
smartphone's pixels! This will give
you a sense of how lots of dots can
create an image.

The first *Super Mario* game
released in 1985
(256 × 240 pixels)

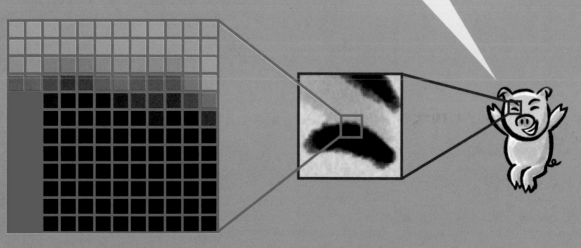

Zoom zoom zoom!

4

The Hanmoji Family

Introducing Your
Favorite Neighbors,
the Hanmojis!

Mommy, I want a pet pig!

Cast of Characters

This radical is never used alone, but the pronunciation is still useful to know as a way to reference the radical.

 宀 **mián**
min4

radical: roof

 人 **rén**
jan4

person, people, human

 女 **nǔ**
neoi5

woman, girl, female

 女

Think of this character as a woman sitting and crossing her legs.

 男 **nán**
naam4

man, boy, male

子 **zǐ**
zi2

child

 豬 猪 **zhū**
zyu1

pig

radical form of "pig":

豕

zhū/zyu1

Language from the Scholarly Class

▶ **Linguistics** is the study of language, including its structural features, such as the way a language works, sounds, and functions, along with its social features, such as the role it plays in society, who defines its terms, and how societal assumptions enter into language. Linguists study language to learn more about different cultures, time periods, and ways of living and seeing the world.

Languages are never neutral; rather, they reveal the values of the society in which they were created and function. Take the words *husband* and *wife* in English, for example. The word *husband* comes from Old English and Norse expressions meaning "head of the household," whereas *wife* derives from the Old English word for "woman." Even if we don't mean the same thing today when we talk about husbands and wives, the history of these words captures an old assumption that wives are simply women whereas husbands are heads of households. There's also the English word *villain*, which comes from the Latin word *villa*, meaning a country house or farm, signaling city dwellers' fear of people from the countryside. And *sinister*, which comes from the Latin *sinistra*, meaning "left," perhaps draws on an ancient belief that the left side represented bad luck since most people are right-handed and therefore have weaker left hands.

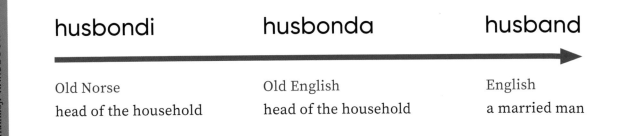

husbondi	husbonda	husband
Old Norse	Old English	English
head of the household	head of the household	a married man

Chinese script has its own assumptions baked into the language, too. Most of Chinese writing was shaped by a scholarly class, who were historically all men. In fact, throughout early Chinese history, women were barred from attending schools and getting an education. Wealthy women and girls could learn to read at home, depending on their access to books and resources. This all but ensured that literate men with power and influence shaped the evolution of the written language. The examples in this chapter help us see how traditional ideas about family entered the written language.

Female Scholars of Early China

Although it was an uphill struggle, a minority of women who were mostly from affluent backgrounds fought to become important writers, poets, and historians.

One of the first female scholars that we have records of is Ban Zhao. She was the coauthor of the definitive history of the early Han dynasty, on top of her other writings in philosophy and poetry.

Ban Zhao is often compared to Pamphile of Epidaurus, in ancient Greece. They are both heralded as the first female historians of their respective lands, and both lived during the first century CE.

Let's Learn Some More Words!

人   person, people, human

rén

jan4

從 从   from, follow, obey

cóng

cung4

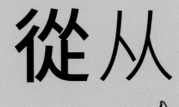

Remember: The bold character on the left is Traditional Chinese, and the one on the right is Simplified Chinese.

眾 众   crowd, many, numerous

zhòng

zung3

人
I'm just a person crossing the street
从
I'm a person following another person crossing the street
These two only work in Simplified Chinese.
众
We're a crowd of persons crossing the street

好

good

hǎo

hou2

One of the most frequently typed characters, *hǎo* technically means "good" but can stand in for "OK," "all right," or a simple word of acknowledgment, like "k." The character consists of a woman (女 *nǚ/noei5*) with a child (子 *zǐ/zi2*), which you might type with two emoji, or a single emoji of a mother and child.

good   child

孖

mā

maa1

twins, a pair

This character is two children side by side. It can also mean "producing many offspring."

What! There's no character for two pigs side by side?

字

zì

zi6

word, character, script

Place a roof (宀 *mián/min4*) over a child (子 *zǐ/zi2*) and what do you get? A Chinese character, of course! In this case, 子 is acting as a phonetic radical, helping you pronounce *zì/zi6*. If you 打字 (*dǎzì/daa2zi6*), or "hit a character," you're typing. How about 字母 (*zìmǔ/zi6mou5*)? It literally means "character mom," but in this case, it means "letter of the alphabet."

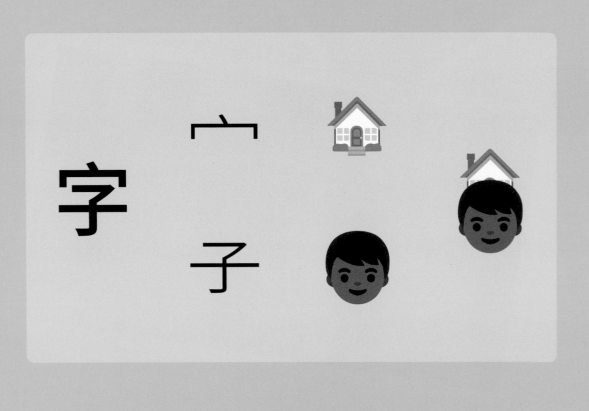

安

ān

on1

peace, comfort, safety

Meaning both "peace" and "comfort," 安 is a roof over a woman. It's hard to know why this particular symbolism emerged for "peace." It could mean that a woman with a roof over her head feels safe and at peace. And in ancient times, a woman was traditionally in charge of the house, which included making it a relaxing and peaceful space.

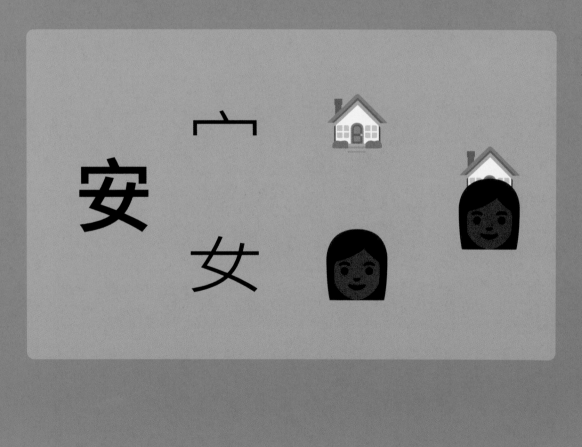

家

jiā

gaa1

home, family

Pigs have a negative connotation in much of the world and are banned in halal and kosher food traditions. But in traditional Chinese society, pigs symbolize a stable home and farm, so much so that the word for "home" shows a pig under a roof. The pig is also one of the twelve zodiac animals, and it symbolizes luck and prosperity. Those born in the Year of the Pig are said to be honest and helpful.

marry

jià

gaa3

In the ancient times when this character was developed and in some cultures today, the only time a woman moves out of her home is when she gets married. The character looks like a woman (女 *nǚ*/*noei5*) outside the home (家 *jiā*/*gaa1*), and it means to "marry into" a family. However, this word can only be used when a woman gets married—there's a different word when a man is married.

In this character, 家 acts more as a phonetic component, indicating that the word is pronounced *jià*/*gaa3*. But it also creates an image of a woman outside a home, getting ready to enter the new home she will share with her partner.

嫁   女 家

5
Mix and Match

Review

▶ Let's review our hanmoji building blocks.

THE FIVE ELEMENTS

🌲	木	mù/muk6	wood
🔥	火	huǒ/fo2	fire
💧	水	shuǐ/seoi2	water; radical form: 氵
🌍	土	tǔ/tou2	earth, soil
🏛	金	jīn/gam1	metal, gold

THE HANMOJI FAMILY

🏠	宀	mián/min4	radical for roof
🧍	人	rén/jan4	person, people, human; radical form: 亻
👩	女	nǔ/neoi5	woman, girl, female
👨	男	nán/naam4	man, boy, male
👦	子	zǐ/zi2	child
🐷	豬/猪	zhū/zyu1	pig; radical form: 豕

Characters are sometimes squeezed and stretched into a radical form, even though they keep the same basic shape.

Now to Mix and Match

▶ With just a few basic parts, like the five elements and the hanmoji family, we can create even more characters and stories. That's part of the magic of logographic languages: building on what you have to create new words and meanings.

The English language is not so different. You can combine *cup* and *board* to make *cupboard*, meaning a place to store not just cups but also plates, bowls, and glasses. This is an example of a **compound word**, in which two words are combined to create a new one.

English also has **portmanteaus**, or words that are made from combining parts of other words. The word *smog*, for example, is *smoke* and *fog* mashed together, and *motel* combines *motor* and *hotel*, because it originally referred to hotels along interstate highways. (The word *hanmoji* is a portmanteau, too! Do you remember which words it combines?) Languages often create new terms by blending or mixing pieces of existing words.

What about emoji? Put on your thinking cap as you learn these hanmoji, and we bet you'll be thinking about creative emoji mash-ups in no time.

Can you guess these common compound words in English based on their emoji?

Answers: mailbox, snowman, sunflower

坐

zuò

z06

sit, seat

Remember 土 (*tǔ*/*tou2*)? It means "earth" or "soil." Put two 人 (*rén*/*jan4*), or people, on top and they're sitting together. In ancient times, people who sat together were usually sitting on the floor. Today, people in China often sit together on low stools to eat yummy street food or gather for a family meal.

坐 ⅄土人

休

xiū

jau1

rest, stop

Feeling tired? Lean your back up against a tree (木 *mù/muk6*) and take a little break. A person (人 *rén/jan4*) next to a tree (木 *mù/muk6*) means "to rest." Xiu is also a last name.

Remember that 亻 is the radical form for "person": 人.

休 亻木

伙

huǒ

fo2

companion, partner, group

Before electricity, getting together often meant sitting around a fire. In this word, the 火 (*huǒ/fo2*) on the right-hand side indicates the sound, but it's also a helpful image. If you're sitting alone by the fire, hopefully someone will join you soon!

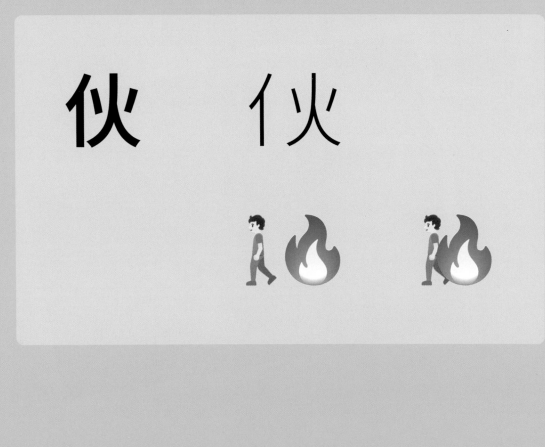

zāi

zoi1

calamity, disaster, personal misfortune

Uh-oh! Is there a fire in your house? This character spells disaster. The Simplified Chinese version of this word is easily confused with 滅/灭 (miè/mit6), which means "extinguish." Look carefully, and you'll see a fire in both, but one has the roof radical and the other is a single line that's extinguishing the fire. In Traditional Chinese, the top radical is 巛, a variant of 川 (chuān/cyun1), or "river." (Can you see the streams of water flowing to make a pictogram of a river?) The radical refers to floods, as fires and floods are common natural disasters.

李

lǐ

lei5

plum, a surname

What's the child of a tree? A plum! Plum trees grow throughout southern China and have been an important crop for centuries. They symbolize hope and strength because they bloom in the winter, against the falling snow. Li is also one of the most common surnames in the world. There are many famous people with the last name Li, which is also romanized as Lee.

Jet Li

Bruce Lee

actors and martial artists

Li Na

tennis star

plum

fruit

Li Qingzhao

Li Bai

Song and Tang dynasty poets

star authors Jason Li and Jennifer 8. Lee!

Song Dynasty

sòng

sung3

Place a roof over a tree and what do you get? The answer isn't so intuitive. This word means "Song," but not the kind you sing. In the tenth century CE, Emperor Taizu of Song, a former military general, established the Song dynasty. During this time, China began using paper money and movable type and established a permanent navy.

宋 is an example of a character with components that don't hint at its sound or its meaning. Today, it's a surname used by people of Chinese, Korean, and Vietnamese descent.

The Soong sisters (*Soong* is another way to transliterate *Song*) were an important trio in the early founding of the Republic of China. At the time, they were the richest women in China and some of the first Chinese women to study in the United States. During a time of political turmoil in China, Ei-ling and May-ling strategized for the Nationalist Party, while Ching-ling worked for the Communist Party. They also married powerful figures: Ching-ling was the wife of Sun Yat-sen, the father of modern China, and May-ling was the wife of Chiang Kai-shek, a general who served as president of the Republic of China. Together, the sisters helped shaped history with their influence on modern China.

Hanmoji Quiz

▶ Match each question on the left with a Chinese character or hanmoji on the right.

Three radicals make up a seat. One of them appears twice. What is the other one?

What is the name of a rare-earth mineral that burns up when heated?

Which of the five elements looks very different in its radical form?

What is the surname Li a "child" of?

How many people does it take to follow someone?

Two of which element will make your body ache?

What's found in the character for all Chinese homes?

Answers from top to bottom:

Hanmoji Pairings

▶ Below are some Chinese characters along with their English definitions. Which emoji do you think works best for each one?

[ ]	心	**xīn** sam1	heart
[ ]	山	**shān** saan1	mountain
[ ]	耳	**ěr** ji5	ear
[ ]	力	**lì** lik6	power, force
[ ]	車车	**chē** ce1	car, vehicle
[ ]	馬马	**mǎ** maa5	horse

6
The Vast World of Hanmoji

Hanmoji Incoming!

▶ Have you ever called a dumpling a little dragon bun or thought of a computer as an electric brain? One of the joys of learning a language is gaining a new perspective. The words we use help shape the way we see the world around us.

In this section, we're dipping our toes into more complicated Chinese forms of expression, from tea to ancient poetry. These phrases include more than one character, and sometimes many. Don't worry too much about trying to memorize everything. The examples here don't always use the building blocks from previous chapters; they're meant to give you a small view into the vast world of hanmoji.

Ready to dive in?

Buckle up, friends! Some big hanmoji are coming your way.

Chinese Idioms Are a Piece of Cake

▶ Learning a language is tough, but it's not rocket science. So hang in there and try to enjoy it, because time flies when you're having fun!

"It's not rocket science," "hang in there," and "time flies" are all examples of **idioms**. Idioms are commonly used phrases that mean more than their literal definition. We're not actually hanging from the monkey bars, and time can't really fly.

In Chinese, **chengyu** are idiomatic phrases. Some are common sayings, references to history, or quotes from famous people or poems.

Most chengyu are made up of four characters. Why is that? The simplest answer is that they sound good in Chinese, forming a rhythm that's pleasant to the ear. They're short enough to be memorable and long enough to say something interesting. In fact, four-character forms have been popular for thousands of years.

In the world of hanmoji, chengyu are a fun way to see the world from a Chinese speaker's perspective.

成語
成语
chéng yǔ

sing4 jyu5

木耳

mù ěr

muk6 ji5

wood ear mushroom

This character literally means "wood ear," and it refers to a type of mushroom popular in Chinese food. The mushroom got its name because it looks like a little ear growing out of a tree. Order hot and sour soup from your local Chinese restaurant, and you're bound to find these dark, skinny mushrooms floating around in it. Yum!

電腦
电脑

diàn nǎo

din6 nou5

computer

Need to use your computer? Just fire up your electric brain and get cracking! In Chinese, the word for electricity, or 電/电 (*diàn/din6*), is used to describe lots of electronic devices. For example:

"electric speech"
telephone

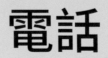

diàn huà

din6 waa2

"electric mail"
email

diàn yóu

din6 jau4

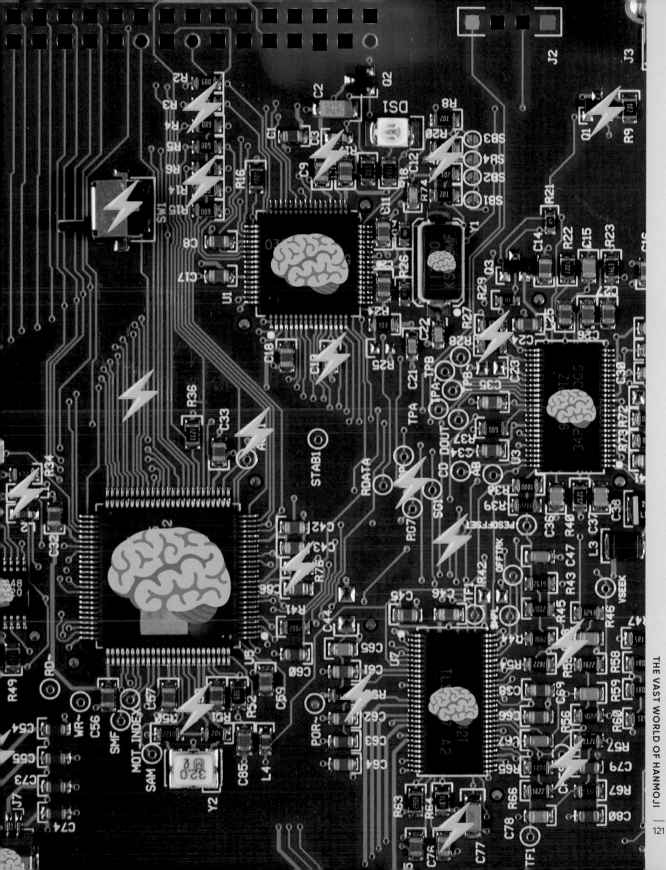

小籠包
小笼包

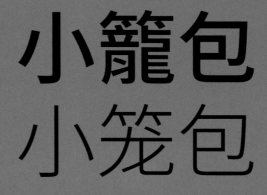

xiǎo lóng bāo

siu2 lung4 baau1

xiaolongbao (a kind of steamed bun)

Here, the three characters for this delicious soup dumpling directly translate to "little," "steamer basket" (which includes radicals for *dragon* and *bamboo*), and "bun." To remember them, think of a little dragon trapped beneath a bamboo steamer, whose fiery breath cooks a delicious bun. Together, they become the beloved *xiaolongbao*, or Shanghai soup dumpling, now popular throughout the world.

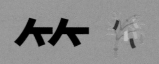

This is the bamboo radical.

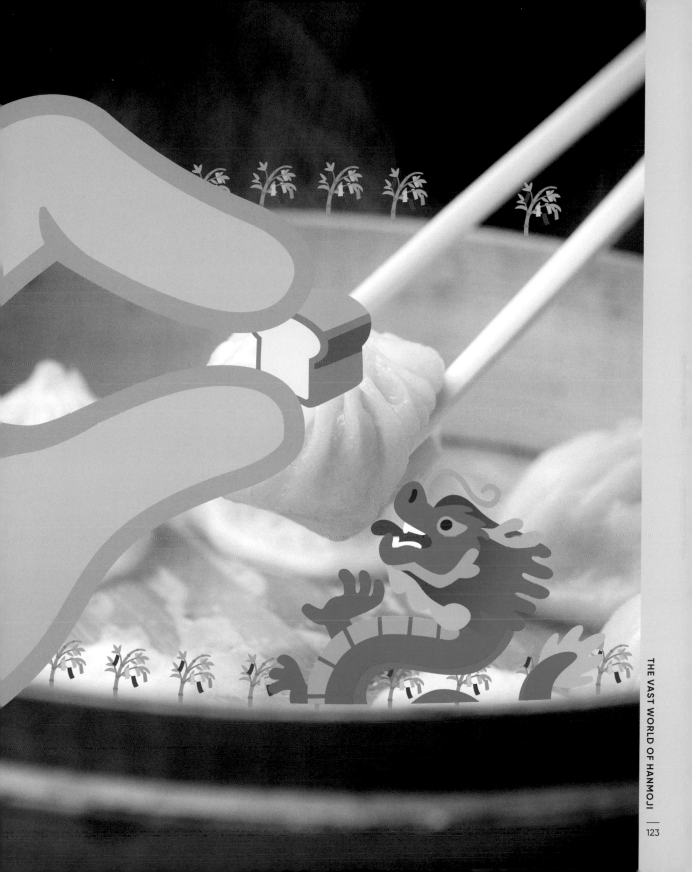

馬馬虎虎
马马虎虎

mǎ mǎ hū hū

maa5 maa5 fu2 fu2

barely good enough, so-so

Legend has it, some people in a village asked an artist to paint a horse. Others asked him to paint a tiger. To split the difference, he painted a mash-up of a horse and a tiger, making an odd picture of an animal that was neither one nor the other and not much of anything.

茶馬古道
茶马古道

chá mǎ gǔ dào

caa4 maa5 gu2 dou6

Old Tea Horse Road

Would you like a cup of tea in exchange for a horse? In the tenth century, trade began between China's southwestern Sichuan province and Tibet, an arduous journey that could take six months or more, through nearly 1,500 miles (2,250 kilometers) of mountains and rivers. This route became known as the Old Tea Horse Road and expanded to other parts of Asia.

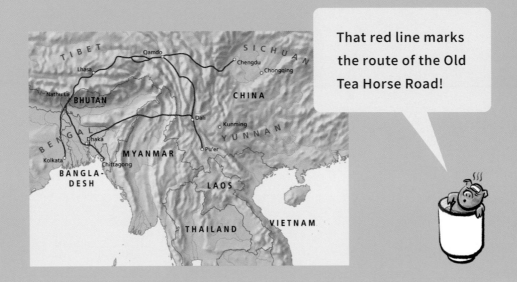

That red line marks the route of the Old Tea Horse Road!

Tea was so valued in chilly Lhasa, the capital of Tibet, that about 130 pounds (60 kilograms) of high-quality tea was worth one horse. The tea was often dried and packaged into cakes that were easy to standardize, transport, and measure, like giant coins.

Today, China is still the world's largest tea producer, exporting different varieties of tea to every country on earth. Sichuan makes some of the world's most prized tea, especially pu'er (普洱 *pǔ'ěr/pou2nei2*), a dark, earthy tea. Today, we pay for tea with money, not horses, but the tea is delicious all the same!

Did You Know?

Remember how there are many Chinese languages? Several of the world's languages refer to tea using either the word *cha* or *te* as its base. In Spanish, for instance, it's called *té* and in French it's *thé*, while in Hindi, Persian, and Swahili, it's called *chai*. This reflects historic trade routes—tea that traveled along the Old Silk Road came with the northern Chinese word *cha*. Meanwhile, Dutch traders brought tea by boat to other parts of the world, using the word *tee* from Min Nan Chinese speakers in the south.

畫龍點睛
画龙点睛

huà lóng diǎn jīng

waak6 lung4 dim2 zing1

paint a dragon dot in the eyes

You can spend ages painting a beautiful dragon, and to wrap it up, you'll have to dab the last dot in its eyes. This phrase refers to the finishing touch, the thing that ties it all together, and the crucial stroke that brings a work to life. In one popular story, when an artist added eyes to a dragon painting, the dragon came alive.

Stop poking me in the eye!

人山人海

rén shān rén hǎi

jan4 saan1 jan4 hoi2

mountains and seas of people

China has many people, mountains, and waters. If a place is crowded, you say "people mountain people sea," or, more idiomatically in English, "mountains and seas of people." Finding colorful words to describe crowds is common across languages. In English, we might say that people in a full train car are "packed like sardines," or that a crowded stadium is "bursting at the seams."

Gives a new meaning to *crowd surfing*, doesn't it?

床前明月光

chuáng qián míng yuè guāng

cong4 cin4 ming4 jyut6 gwong1

"In front of my bed, the light of the bright moon"

This is one of the most famous lines of traditional Chinese poetry, written by Li Bai (more popularly known as Li Po from an earlier romanization system), a towering poet equivalent to Shakespeare. Starting from when they are very young, Chinese students memorize poetry, and many adults can still recite the full poem from which this line is taken; it's called "Quiet Night Thoughts" (靜夜思 *jìngyèsī/zing6je6si1*) and contains many coded references, rhymes, puns, and turns of phrase.

The character 明 (*míng*), meaning "light," is a combination of the characters 日 (*rì*) and 月 (*yuè*), "sun" and "moon."

尋尋覓覓冷冷清清
寻寻觅觅冷冷清清

xúnxún mìmì lěnglěng qīngqīng

cam4 cam4 mik6 mik6 laang5 laang5 cing1 cing1

"Searching searching seeking seeking cold cold clear clear"

Li Qingzhao wrote both poems and essays during the Song dynasty, a time when women were not allowed to attend school, but could get an education at home if they were of the upper class. While the most famous historic poets in China are men from the Tang and Song dynasties, Li Qingzhao is one of the few female poets whose words are widely known and studied today.

These are the opening lines of her famous poem "Sound Sound Slow" (sometimes translated as "Slow, Slow Song," 聲聲慢 *shēngshēngmàn/sing1sing1maan6*), a reflection on her sadness after the death of her husband. It's written in the **ci form**, a type of formal poetry that was written to a set of poetic meters and meant to be sung.

空山不見人
空山不见人

kōng shān bú jiàn rén

hung1 saan1 bat1 gin3 jan4

"On the empty mountain, I see no one"

This is the first line of the poet Wang Wei's "Deer Park" (鹿柴 *lùchái/luk6caai4*), a famous Tang dynasty poem. It's written in the **shanshui** ("mountains and rivers," 山水 *shānshuǐ/saan1seoi2*) tradition, which means it's designed to evoke a painting or an image.

Wang Wei's poem was heavily shaped by a school of Buddhism called Chan Buddhism, with influences from Daoism. Chan emphasizes direct experience of reality through meditation, and Chan poetry often suggests reality through subtle descriptions. When Chan Buddhism spread to Japan, it became known as Zen.

7

The Future

Boba and Biang: A Tale of Two Snacks

▶ In 2020, two snacks were added to Unicode by the Unicode Consortium. The emoji for bubble tea, also known as **boba**, was included thanks to three enterprising people who wanted this beloved Taiwanese drink, a mix of tea, milk, and tapioca balls, accessible on keyboards.

The consortium also made the character for **biang**, a kind of long, flat noodle popular in Shaanxi, China, available in Unicode. The noodles have been made for three thousand years, and the character is epic, taking an amazing fifty-six strokes to draw. Nobody knows for sure who invented this character. Some people say that it was created by a member of Emperor Qin's court. Others say it was first used by a student trying to get out of paying a bill. Meanwhile, the realists believe that it simply started at an enterprising noodle shop.

biáng

While the character can be found on many noodle shops in the region, it wasn't in most dictionaries. So in early 2020, a group within the Shaanxi Provincial Department of Culture and Tourism started an initiative to add the character to modern Chinese dictionaries. Unrelated to this initiative, the Unicode Consortium accepted the character two months later, after many years of discussion and reviews of multiple proposals.

In the same way you invented your own hanmoji earlier, Chinese speakers around the world are playing with and inventing new Chinese characters every day. Often they're combining existing radicals to generate new meanings. Most of the time, these new characters remain an inside joke among a group of friends or are used only once in a printed advertisement. But occasionally, the new character resonates with lots of people and spreads until it becomes an official part of the written Chinese language.

Whether it's a new emoji or a new Chinese character, the official process for approval on computers, phones, and other digital devices still ends at the Unicode Consortium, where designers and technologists have to figure out the code to make sure these words can be used worldwide. In the case of bubble tea, a group originally proposed putting together the existing emoji for tea, milk, and a black ball to encode the emoji. This would have made it faster to add to emoji keyboards. In the end, however, they decided to give bubble tea—and biang—their own code points. No matter how complex an illustration, its code point (the number that gives a character an identity in Unicode) is simple and efficient to transfer across the internet.

Thanks to the work of designers, computer scientists, and creative, food-loving people, Chinese language and emoji keyboards all over the world now have bubble tea and biang.

WHO GETS TO DECIDE ON NEW WORDS AND TERMS IN CHINESE?
Here are some of the key players:

A Dictionary of Current Chinese, compiled by the Chinese Academy of Social Sciences and published by the Commercial Press, in Beijing, China

The Unihan Database at the Unicode Consortium, based in Mountain View, California

The Linguistic Society of Hong Kong, an academic nonprofit organization

The Ministry of Education, Taiwan

Chinese Culture Immortalized in Emoji

▶ Since the late 1990s, a handful of Chinese cultural symbols have made their way into emoji form.

Mooncakes (月餅/月饼 *yuèbǐng/jyut6beng2*) are a delicious treat that pop up once a year during the Mid-Autumn Festival. Legend has it that during the Yuan dynasty, small slips of paper containing secret messages were hidden inside mooncakes.

Red envelopes (紅包/红包 *hóngbāo/hung4baau1* or 利是 *lìshì/lai6si6*), also known as ang pao, hóngbāo, and lai see, are typically exchanged between family and friends during the Lunar New Year, which falls about one to two months after January 1. What's inside the envelope? Cash, the most practical and direct gift!

Fortune cookies (簽語餅/签语饼 *qiānyǔbǐng/cim1jyu5beng2*) are an end-of-meal snack at Chinese restaurants all over the United States. Fun fact: people don't serve fortune cookies in China, which is why they are such a quintessential Chinese American symbol.

Dumplings (餃子/饺子 *jiǎozi/gaau2zi2*) may be popular among Chinese people, but dumplings of one kind or another are a part of almost every cuisine in the world. Think about it—a dumpling is really just yummy goodness wrapped in a layer of dough, whether fried, steamed, baked, or boiled.

One of the authors of this book wrote another book called *The Fortune Cookie Chronicles*, which talks about how the fortune cookie was likely invented by Japanese people!

How Emoji Are Born

▶ Anyone can submit an emoji proposal to the Unicode Consortium, but only a small fraction of proposals are accepted because the Unicode Consortium adds a limited number of emoji each year. To make a compelling case for a new emoji, you need two things. First, you have to supply a design—in both color and black and white—that looks different from any current emoji. Then you have to answer questions about why your proposed emoji is culturally relevant, how popular it would be, whether or not the emoji has any double meanings, and where it would fit on the emoji keyboard.

An emoji proposal can fail to advance because it lacks demonstrated longevity (a lesson learned from the pager emoji), it's too close to an existing emoji (do we need a cooked turkey if we already have a live turkey?), or the concept it represents is hard to show in a small space (emoji need to be visually distinguishable in a text message).

If you choose to submit a proposal, the Unicode Emoji Subcommittee will review it. Very few proposals will make it through the entire process, and often only after the subcommittee has asked for revisions, such as an improved image or further evidence about its cultural relevance and projected popularity. Only once in a while does a proposal sail through in its original form.

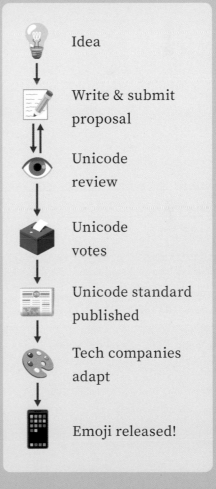

Idea

Write & submit proposal

Unicode review

Unicode votes

Unicode standard published

Tech companies adapt

Emoji released!

The subcommittee uses a process of consensus building to decide whether a proposed emoji meets their requirements. If it does, they give it their stamp of approval. The next step is for the entire Unicode Technical Committee to vote on giving the emoji a place in the Unicode Standard. If a proposal passes that final hurdle, then a new emoji is on its way to reaching billions of people.

After Unicode approves the emoji, it's up to the technology companies to adopt and adapt it. Starting from the guidelines on basic appearance and design published by the Unicode Consortium, companies spend months designing the new emoji for their platforms and devices. They also give the new emoji names in most of the major languages used today. When the companies finally release their versions of the new emoji, it often makes newspaper headlines around the globe.

Sauna Emoji: Proposed versus Published

When you propose an emoji, you draw a picture of what you think it should look like. But sometimes the final emoji doesn't look exactly the way you first drew it.

Amid the fanfare, what's often not obvious is the amount of work and time—sometimes up to two years!—that it takes for an emoji to go through the process of approval, review, design, and release.

The Rise of Inclusive Emoji

Over the years, Unicode has tried to make emoji more diverse and representative of the world around us—in large part because emoji users demanded it. When Unicode introduced its first set of emoji in 2010, it was a very limited set compared with what we have today. There was only one skin color for all emoji, which was often set as yellow (or on some operating systems, a monstrous gray!). And its meager attempts at cultural representation, which it inherited from the emoji made by Japanese phone companies, included images based on racial stereotypes.

Since then, much effort has been made to broaden the emoji set to be more inclusive of people, animals, and foods from all around the world. Many of these ideas came from users who were passionate about seeing themselves on the emoji keyboard. For example, we now have five new skin tones thanks to a Black entrepreneur from Texas named Katrina Parrott, whose daughter came home one day and asked for an emoji that looked like her.

Similarly, the hijab emoji was proposed by a fifteen-year-old Saudi Arabian girl named Rayouf Alhumedhi, who wanted an emoji to represent the millions of girls and women who wear the hijab. A type designer at Adobe, Paul Hunt, wanted emoji for people who are gender nonbinary—so now we have several non-gender-binary emoji, including a merperson and Mx. Claus emoji! And Apple successfully proposed a slate of emoji to represent people who are deaf, are blind, or use wheelchairs.

Learning the Future . . . through the Past

▶ Will the future of emoji follow in the footsteps of the Chinese language? With eighty thousand Chinese characters and just three thousand emoji, there's a lot more room for new emoji, even while some fall into disuse.

dǐng
ding2

optical disc or "CD"

The character 鼎, meaning a vessel or cauldron, used to be common. Today, cooking with a pot or wok is much more typical, so the old character has fallen out of use and mostly just survives in idioms.

Similarly, CDs were everywhere in the 1990s, but fewer and fewer people use them today. So that emoji is no longer seen as frequently.

Even while some emoji and Chinese characters go out of date, they sometimes find a new life in another form. The character 戈 (gē/gwo1), meaning battle-ax, is rarely used these days in everyday conversation. But it lives on in idioms related to fighting and conflicts, and in characters like 找 (zhǎo/zaau2), which means "find" or "seek." Similarly, the floppy disk emoji lives on as a "save" icon in many software programs, even if few people use real floppy disks to save files anymore.

When I was young . . .

By looking at how the Chinese language has changed over thousands of years, we might find hints about the future of emoji.

Born 2003   Born 2010   Born 2020

For example, emoji are already being combined to form new emoji, just as Chinese characters combine to form new words.

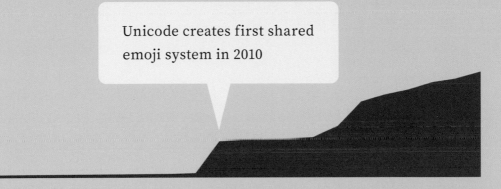

Unicode creates first shared emoji system in 2010

176 emoji in 1999   3,535 emoji in 2021

The number of emoji grows every year. Do you think we'll ever reach a point where we are commonly using thousands of emoji in our communication?

Chinese characters changed a lot during their early years but have settled down to look more or less the same over the past thousand years. Will emoji eventually stop changing and become standardized across all platforms?

The Future of Emoji Is Up to Us

▶ What will emoji look like in a hundred years? In a thousand? How about three thousand? The great thing about emoji is that we all have a hand in growing and developing them. Here are a few ideas!

- Use emoji in creative ways. The more frequently emoji are used, remixed, and repurposed, the more they take on a life of their own. Can you come up with new meanings for your favorite emoji? Are there emoji you wish other people used more?

- Make emoji art and drawings. Bring emoji into your creative work. Emoji belong to all of us, and they can be combined and shared.

- Propose your own emoji to the Unicode Consortium! It takes some work and research, but new emoji are made all the time thanks to people like you writing up proposals and sharing their ideas.

The future of emoji is up to us and how we imagine them and build them as a form of communication. The story of emoji is just getting started.

Join the Emoji Story: Emoji Proposal Starter Pack

▶ Want to try drawing a new emoji? Take out a blank piece of paper and draw a square in the middle of it. Inside the square, sketch out your idea for a new emoji. Try to keep the lines simple, like a cartoon, so that it's easy to identify from afar. Look at what emoji are out there, and make sure that what you draw doesn't look like something that already exists. If you add color to your drawing, remember to use distinct colors that are both light and dark, so the image stands out.

Make an emoji of me!

Wait, there are already *three* pig emoji? And a boar, too?

Turn over your piece of paper and write down the answers to these prompts:

- What's the name of your emoji?

- What are five reasons your emoji is important enough to reach billions of phones and computers? If your emoji is very important to a specific place or group of people, or if a lot of people are asking for your emoji in a petition or news article, include those as reasons.

- Pull out an emoji keyboard on a smartphone and find out where your new emoji would go. Which emoji should it be next to?

- Explain why you can't just use existing emoji to represent your new emoji. If your emoji is passed, how might it be combined with existing emoji to represent a concept or phrase?

- Run an internet search on the name of your emoji. How many search results does it have? Does it have more search results than "elephant"?

"Elephant" has served as a standard search, because the elephant emoji is of average popularity.

I'm a greater-than-average emoji if you ask me!

That's it! Now you're well on your way to finishing an emoji proposal. For the latest guidelines on submitting to the Unicode Consortium, run an internet search on "Unicode submitting emoji proposal," or visit www.emojination.org.

The Future of Hanmoji

▶ One of the most amazing things about emoji is that they are regularly being created. And as new emoji form, new hanmoji become possible. Since the Unicode Consortium approves a number of emoji for the world's devices each year, in a year or two, there will be even more emoji available.

The spirit of hanmoji is all about playing with emoji in creative ways to make it easier and more fun to learn the Chinese language. This book has just a small number of examples from thousands of Chinese characters. There are countless compound words, idioms, characters, and poems left to learn, and as your language journey continues, you can use all of the many emoji at your fingertips to help you remember Chinese words—and maybe even learn a little history while you're at it. Language is always evolving and changing as people experiment and find new ways to express themselves.

The future of hanmoji starts now, using your brain, your electric brain, and just a little bit of elbow grease.

So long, or as some people say, 拜拜 (*báibái/bai1bai1*)!

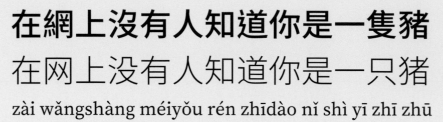

在網上沒有人知道你是一隻豬

在网上没有人知道你是一只猪

zài wǎngshàng méiyǒu rén zhīdào nǐ shì yī zhī zhū

zoi6 mong5 seong6 mut6 jau5 jan4 zi1 dou3 nei5 si6 jat1 zek3 zyu1

On the internet, nobody knows you're a pig.

Acknowledgments

In the ultimate act of filial piety (孝 *xiào/haau3*), the authors would like to first and foremost offer thanks to our respective parents, siblings, and extended family members, and to our teachers and professors who nurtured our love of language. We're sorry we couldn't get A+s on every Chinese exam, but we hope this book makes up for it.

The Hanmoji Handbook would have been impossible without Yilin Wang, who provided essential Mandarin Chinese language and history fact-checking. We are also grateful to Xiaowei Wang and Shlo for their everlasting moral support, and John Stith and Hrag Vartanian for their early editorial input.

We are grateful to the Unicode, Unicode Emoji Subcommittee, and Emojination communities for supporting our early exploration of these ideas and to MITeen Press and Candlewick Press, including Amy Brand, Karen Lotz, Olivia Swomley, Hannah Mahoney, Phoebe Kosman, Vera Villanueva, Matt Roeser, and Nancy Brennan, for shepherding us through this book's creation. And we want to thank the designers and artists behind the Noto Emoji project—we hope you take great joy in your art being part of hanmoji learning.

Bibliography

Buchholz, Katharina. "The History of the 5 Billion Emojis Used Every Single Day." World Economic Forum. September 30, 2020. https://www.weforum.org/agenda/2020/09/emoji-numbers -facts-social-media-how-many-twitter-facebook-instagram/.

"Chinese Research and Bibliographic Methods for Beginners: Romanization." UNC University Libraries. Last updated June 25, 2021. https://guides.lib.unc.edu/chinese_bib/romanization.

Chow, Bun Ching. *Cantonese for Everyone (Jyutping version)*. Hong Kong: Commercial Press, 2009.

Fan, Jiayang. "The Famous, Feuding Siblings Who Helped Shape Modern China." *New York Times*, October 29, 2019. https://www.nytimes.com/2019/10/29/books/review/big-sister-little-sister-red -sister-jung-chang.html.

Galloway, Paul. "The Original NTT DOCOMO Emoji Set Has Been Added to the Museum of Modern Art's Collection." Museum of Modern Art. October 26, 2016. https://stories.moma.org /the-original-emoji-set-has-been-added-to-the-museum-of-modern-arts-collection-c6060e141f61.

Ho, Olivia. "Love, Loss and Legacy of the Soong Sisters." *Straits Times*, November 26, 2019. https:// www.straitstimes.com/lifestyle/love-loss-and-legacy-of-the-soong-sisters.

Moser, David. *A Billion Voices: China's Search for a Common Language*. London: Penguin, 2016.

National Museums Scotland. "Oracle Bones." https://www.nms.ac.uk/explore-our-collections /stories/world-cultures/oracle-bones/.

Shashkevich, Alex. "The Power of Language: How Words Shape People, Culture." *Stanford News*, August 22, 2019. https://news.stanford.edu/2019/08/22/the-power-of-language-how-words-shape -people-culture/.

Sigley, Gary. "The Ancient Tea Horse Road: The Politics of Cultural Heritage in Southwest China." *China Heritage Quarterly* 29 (March 2012), 1–6.

Wang, Yang. "Introduction to Chinese Characters." Brown University Year of China. https://www .brown.edu/about/administration/international-affairs/year-of-china/language-and-cultural -resources/introduction-chinese-characters/introduction-chinese-characters.

Image Credits

Unless otherwise stated, emoji are in Noto font.

p. 5: Pixabay/Brett Sayles (top left), Pixabay (top right), Pexels/Barbara Barbosa (bottom left), Pexels/Peggy Anke (bottom right)

p. 8 (phones): Courtesy of Design at Meta; designs are the intellectual property of their respective owners.

pp. 36 and 56 (photos): Pexels/mali maeder (wood), Pixabay/Ronald Plett (fire), Pixabay/Dean Moriarty (earth), Pixabay/Harry Strauss (metal), Pixabay/Charles Rondeau (water)

p. 43 (ancient characters): Wiktionary

p. 47 (photos): Pixabay/Pavlofox (top), Pixabay/Wolfgang Claussen (middle), Pixabay/Free-Photos (bottom)

p. 49 (photo): Pexels/mali maeder

p. 51 (photo): Pixabay/Benedict Rottmann

p. 53 (photos): Jumk.de Webprojects, *Ultrapure holmium, 17 grams*, original size: 1.5 cm x 2.5 cm, 2016, Creative Commons Attribution 3.0 Unported License, retrieved from https://images-of-elements.com/holmium.php

p. 55 (photos): Pexels/Vladyslav Dukhin (top), Pixabay/Ylvers (bottom)

p. 60 (Emperor Qin and leftmost character): Wikipedia

p. 61: Pixabay/Thierry Raimbault (top), Wikipedia (middle and bottom)

p. 63: Pixabay/Herbert Bieser

p. 64 (first two columns of characters): Wiktionary

pp. 66 (cat emoji), 67 (angry face emoji), and 69 (dog emoji): Courtesy of Emojipedia, copyright © by their respective creators

p. 70 (stickers): Courtesy of LINE STORE, copyright © by LINE Corporation

pp. 72 and 73 (pixelated bear emoji): Courtesy of Emojipedia, copyright © by its creator

p. 73: Wikipedia (Emperor Qin and leftmost character), Wikipedia/Unicode Consortium (Unicode logo)

p. 75 (game image): Courtesy of Super Mario Wiki, copyright © by Nintendo

p. 81 (Ban Zhao): Wikipedia

p. 83 (crosswalk): Pexels/Donald Tong

p. 85 (photo): Pixabay/Blee James

p. 87 (photos): Pixabay/ID 3194556 (top), Pixabay/学习 黄 (bottom)

p. 89 (photo): Pexels/Marta Wave

p. 91 (photos): Shutterstock/Tara Patta (left), Shutterstock/Phovoir (right)

p. 93 (photo): Shutterstock/Grigvovan

p. 95 (photo): Pixabay/StockSnap

p. 101 (photo): Pixabay/Sarah Richter

p. 103 (photos): Pixabay/Belajati Raihan Fahrizi (top), Pixabay/Dean Moriarty (bottom)

p. 105 (photos): Pixabay/Chris Aram (top), Pixabay/Marcos Aguilar (bottom)

p. 107: Pixabay/Pexels

p. 109: Robert Scoble, *Jet Li, Davos 2009*, Creative Commons Attribution 2.0 Generic license, retrieved from https://commons.wikimedia.org/wiki/File:Jet_Li_2009_(cropped).jpg, Wikipedia/National General Pictures (Bruce Lee), Charlie Cowins, *Li Na at the 2009 US Open*, 2009, Creative Commons Attribution 2.0 Generic license, retrieved from https://commons.wikimedia.org/wiki/File:Li_Na_at_the_2009_US_Open_02.jpg (Li Na), Pixabay/congerdesign (plum), Wikipedia (Li Qingzhao and Li Bai)

p. 111 (photo): Wikipedia/WikiLaurent

p. 119 (photos): Wikipedia/Brücke-Osteuropa (top), Pixabay/Monika Schröder (bottom)

p. 121 (photo): Pexels/Miguel Á. Padriñán

p. 123 (photo): Shutterstock/TMON

p. 125 (painting): Pixabay/Jacques-Laurent Agasse

p. 127 (photo): Shutterstock/lrosebrugh

p. 128: Redgeographics, *Map of the Tea-Horse Road*, 2017, Creative Commons Attribution-Share Alike 4.0 International license, retrieved from https://commons.wikimedia.org/wiki/File:Map_of_the_Tea-Horse_road.png

p. 131 (photo): Pixabay/Hans Braxmeier

p. 133 (photo): Pixabay/MrBin

p. 135 (photo): Shutterstock/FPSO

p. 137 (photo): Pixabay/janeb13

p. 139 (painting): National Palace Museum/Shen Zhou 沈周

p. 142: Wikipedia/Erin Silversmith/Cangjie6 (character), Shutterstock/Claudio Rampinini (photo)

p. 143: Courtesy of Douban, copyright © by 商务印书馆 (dictionary), Courtesy of and copyright © by the Linguistic Society of Hong Kong (bottom left logo), Wikipedia/Unicode Consortium (top right logo), Courtesy of and copyright © by the Ministry of Education, Taiwan (bottom right logo)

p. 145 (Unicode logo): Wikipedia/Unicode Consortium

p. 146: Sauna emoji submission art by Bruno Leo Ribeiro

p. 149: Graph based on Statista, "A Short History of the Emoji," https://www.statista.com/chart/17275/number-of-emojis-from-1995-bis-2019/

Index

Terms in italics indicate a word or phrase for which the Chinese characters are provided.